CHRISTINE CRAFT
AN ANCHORWOMAN'S STORY

Other Rhodora Books published by Capra Press:
LOVE STORY OF THE CENTURY

THE FAMILY SECRET

CHRISTINE CRAFT
An Anchorwoman's Story

By Christine Craft

WITH A FOREWORD BY
Howard Rosenberg

A RHODORA BOOK
Published by Capra Press, Santa Barbara
1986

Copyright ©1986 by Christine Craft.
All rights reserved.
Printed in the United States of America.

Cover by Trish Reynales.
Editorial direction by Marilyn Yalom.
Designed and typeset in Plantin by Jim Cook.

LIBRARY OF CONGRESS CATALOGING IN PUBLICATION DATA
Craft, Christine, 1944-
Christine Craft: an anchorwoman's story.
"A Rhodora book."
  1. Craft, Christine, 1944- —Trials, litigation, etc.
  2. Metromedia, Inc.—Trials, litigation, etc.
  3. Women journalists—Legal status, laws, etc.—Missouri—Kansas City.
  4. Sex discrimination in employment—Law and legislation—
     Missouri—Kansas City.
  5. Sex. discrimination against women—Law and legislation—
     Missouri—Kansas City. I. Title.
KF228.C73C73   1986   345.73′0256   86-9742
ISBN 0-88496-248-2   347.305256
ISBN 0-88496-253-9 (pbk.)

A RHODORA BOOK
Published by Capra Press
Post Office Box 2068
Santa Barbara, California 93120

FOREWORD

"Too ugly?" I could hardly believe what I had been told on the phone.

I first learned about Christine Craft from my mother in Kansas City. We were talking long distance one night in 1981 when she mentioned a Santa Barbara woman who had lost her Kansas City news anchor job "because she was too ugly." This repellent creature who had been banished from KMBC in Kansas City apparently was working again in Santa Barbara, less than an hour's drive from my house in suburban Los Angeles.

An anchorwoman who was "too ugly"? I'd been covering television long enough to know just how much local TV newscasts favored cosmetics over content. Yet this sounded too bizarre to be true. Anchors with bad ratings are routinely discarded like used tissues, but how ugly was too ugly? Quasimodo ugly? The Elephant Man ugly?

Several weeks later, I saw for myself when a Los Angeles TV station interviewed Christine—her fame was spreading—at her rented beach house in Carpinteria, near Santa Barbara. There was no mistaking the woman on the screen for Miss Lip Gloss, but she had the kind of wholesome good looks that most anyone should have found pleasing. If Christine Craft was not attractive enough for TV news, then TV news was in even worse shape than I had thought. And so was my hometown of Kansas City.

It was obvious that Christine would make a terrific story. I called her at KEYT-TV, where she was again anchoring the news after returning from KMBC, and she agreed to an interview.

The first thing I noticed about Christine when she greeted me at the door was that she was prettier in person than she photographed. The second thing I noticed was her dog. He was enormous.

I liked Christine immediately. I liked her sense of humor, her intelligence, her directness, her warmth and how easy she was to be with. I even liked her dog.

The story Christine told me that day was boggling, at once appalling and comical. It was appalling because it revealed TV news as a grubby bastion of prejudice against females. It was comical because KMBC's obsession with a newscaster's clothes and other cosmetic trivia approached farce.

A station imposing a daily fashion calendar on a female news anchor? Regular wardrobe sessions with a clothing consultant? Give me a break! Give us all a break! What did any of this have to do with the TV news business? Plenty, unfortunately.

It turned out that the issue of Christine's looks was only the tip of the wart, as everyone was to discover from her first trial in Kansas City, which I covered for my paper. More precisely, she accused KMBC of lying when hiring her and discriminating against her because she was female. She also charged KMBC with claiming that it fired her as an anchor because viewers felt she was "too old, too unattractive and not deferential to men."

The facts are that she was thirty-seven at the time, thus hardly decrepit. She was also younger and vastly better looking than the odd-looking KMBC executives who were asking her to become a Barbie doll. As for not deferring to her co-anchor and other males on the set, however, Christine was guilty as charged. Clearly, she was one uppity woman.

Maybe that was the trouble, for Christine—with her agile and independent mind, biting sense of humor, knowledge of sports and seemingly indomitable spirit—was exactly the kind of female whom some men found threatening.

Well, maybe she was less indomitable than she appeared.

I learned a lot about Christine during her first trial. I learned that regardless of the verdict, she would still be a winner because she had the guts to fight back. I learned that she was a populist who loved mingling with the press and courtroom spectators before each day's session. I learned that she was extraordinarily articulate. I learned that she handled adversity well.

I also learned, though, that she was vulnerable beneath her exterior toughness. I saw that side of her on a morning when she could endure no more and left the courtroom as the jury heard a tape of a KMBC focus group interview whose leader described her in a coarse way. I saw it again the evening the verdict came down in her favor. She sat in the kitchen of a friend, her defenses down, her face drawn and haggard, looking defeated and totally spent even though she had won.

Won, temporarily.

I believed Christine's extraordinary story when she first told it to me in Carpinteria. I believed it when I heard it in court. I believe it now. I also believe that she ultimately lost her case the way someone loses a wallet to a pickpocket.

In an offbeat way, though, hers is a story with a happy ending. Since she began her litigation, other women in broadcasting have pushed forward with their own sex bias-related cases, some of them emerging victorious. They should all toast Christine. How could they not have been inspired by her courage?

Are male TV executives getting the message? Perhaps, but it may be the wrong message. Not long after Christine's first trial, I covered a news directors' convention at which a panel discussion was devoted to a review of her case. I expected the male news directors on the panel to at least give lip service to giving females on their staffs equity with male employees. Instead, they discussed how to avoid "bad apples" like Christine in the future.

Some bad apple. On the contrary, Christine is one of those rare TV anchors who is a true journalist, bright, curious and incisive, as much at ease with a pad and pencil as in front of a camera. She remains to this day a work in progress, however, unfinished and unbowed, always testing uncharted waters and exploring new venues. One suspects that there are many more interesting stops in her future. Maybe someday she'll even run for Congress. We can always use a proven winner.

—HOWARD ROSENBERG

1.

I'LL ALWAYS REMEMBER the words: "Christine, our viewer research results are in and they are really devastating. The people of Kansas City don't like watching you anchor the news because you are too old, too unattractive, and you are not sufficiently deferential to men. We know it's silly, but you just don't hide your intelligence to make the guys look smarter. Apparently the people of Kansas City are more provincial than even we had thought. They don't like the fact that you know the difference between the American and the National League! We've decided to remove you from your anchor chair effective immediately. You can stay on and continue your reporting and earn the rest of your contracted salary, but just remember that when the people of Kansas City see your face, they turn the dial."

These blunt statements came at the end of nine months of hell at the hands of a major broadcasting conglomerate, Metromedia, Inc. They had originally hired me saying they loved my "look," appreciated the fact that I was a seasoned journalist, and had no intention of changing me. Since I had not been hired sight unseen, I trusted their initial statements. But from the very beginning of my tenure at their midwestern television station, my attention began to be drawn repeatedly to the fact that my squarish jaw and somewhat uneven eyes made me a less desirable commodity than they had originally thought.

Since it takes a good deal of self-confidence to be an "on-air" person in the first place, I was at first merely puzzled by the emphasis on things I could not change short of major plastic surgery. The men could be balding, jowly, bespectacled, even fat and encased in double-knit, yet the women had to be flawless. Moreover, there was the expectation that I should pretend not to know certain facts just because I was female. The unveiled implication was that not to do so would be unfeminine.

I was not naive. I knew that this breed of sexual discrimination was endemic to the American workplace, not just to broadcasting. Many women would later tell me their own stories of having to train entry-level male employees, who were then given promotions and paid more than the women.

As an eighth-generation American woman who found herself in a business which creates role models for the rest of the culture, I chose to challenge the bigoted mindset that would keep me and other female colleagues in a state of perpetual second-class citizenship. I knew also that by vociferously sticking up for myself I might diminish my chances of remaining in TV news. Had I been a more typical anchorwoman, I probably would have fielded the insults and denial of rights in a more discreet fashion. But I was not typical. And as it turned out, that perhaps made me the right person for the wrong thing to happen to at the right time.

Back in my school days I certainly had been no model collegian. I nonetheless managed to graduate from the University of California at Santa Barbara with a BA in English in 1968. That was the year before the Bank of America in Isla Vista was torched by protestors and an oil company drilling platform blew out, befouling the Santa Barbara Channel. I had cruised through college on one of my slower gears, occupied as I was by a compelling avocation. To me, surfing on Santa Barbara's green glassy winter waves was next to Godliness.

Lest here or anywhere else in my narrative the sport of surfing be dismissed as inconsequential, I have this rejoinder. It is. That's precisely its charm. Only one who has surfed can appreciate its bounty. Sociologists decry the stress of the pace in the modern fast track. Surfing carries the participant through the natural rhythms and speeds of the wave. The sheer thrills involved in this absolve the mind of care, of measured thought, of polluted impressions. Surfing is, by its very anti-intellectuality, an outlet that can provide a joyful release of all that ails you. Nevertheless, a surfer's go-for-it attitude also implies that a full life is not without some degree of risk-taking.

Since I was young and busy taking watery risks, a true sense of academic priorities did not emerge in me until my senior year. Then, studying William Blake, I keyed into the beauties and intricacies of my field of study. But just as I really got turned on, it was time to graduate.

After college I had several years of work experience before I made the jump to television news. I worked for a couple of years at a school for emotionally disturbed teenagers. It was rough, the pay was poor, and it was difficult not to take the job home with me every night. But there were rewards, too. For example, if you were successful in teaching some usually hyperactive fifteen-year-old how to surf, then you could watch her experience rare minutes of relaxed self-expression.

My greatest memories there were of getting the kids to script, produce, and act in two 16mm films. As camerawoman and editor, I had the privilege of seeing some of them who had so much trouble with real life really shine when they had a chance to create. One young girl fraught with very severe epileptic seizures chose to act out an old-time movie. She re-invented Charlie Chaplin, giving every jerky movement subtle meaning.

Another girl, who weighed nearly four hundred pounds, lip-synched perfectly to a tune by the proudly over-abundant Mama Cass. I had never seen this usually miserable girl so happy.

This was also my own first dabbling in the fun of putting pictures and words together. I don't think I had ever enjoyed anything more.

Five years later, approaching thirty, while sitting in the

flower garden of my house in the seaside community of Carmel, I remembered that earlier encounter with filmmaking. I was looking for a career direction that would be something other than retail sales, waitressing, or managing dining rooms—the kinds of jobs I'd taken during the years when I had wanted to be free to enjoy the ocean in the daytime. But now, surfing was no longer the focus of my existence. I was ready for something new.

In a subdued flash of career inspiration, I thought about all the people who presented the local television newscasts. I had the determined feeling that I could do it as well as some of them, perhaps even better than a few.

Armed with that sort of naive self-assurance, I proceeded to write mock broadcasts and record my renditions on a tape recorder. Employing an overly wordy prose style, I soon learned that the format had to be much more precise and condensed.

I talked to my mother, a former actress, who gave me some tips on breath control and modulation of my beginner's monotone. She also sent me tapes of a popular newscaster in Los Angeles, Kelly Lange. Kelly had a very authentic style of speaking, she made you feel that the person you were listening to was not a phony. I soon realized that just being yourself could be much more difficult than it seemed. But I just kept recording and recording, my husband Lorenzo tending radishes and marigolds in the background as I intoned with mock seriousness about make-believe explosions, fires, and political squabbles.

Lorenzo was upbeat and enthusiastic about my news aspirations, never stinting in his encouragement. Our involvement with each other at the time provided a perfect emotional climate for both of us to pursue our dreams. He was the budding young filmmaker, some eight years my junior. A big evening for us was usually when we had the money to rent a Kurosawa or Jean Vigo film. We would screen them over and over, fascinated with the subliminal refinements we discovered in each viewing.

Later we'd drift to sleep under our skylight while listening to strains of Shakespeare from the outdoor theater-in-the-round next door. One summer night we heard the actor playing *Richard the Third* bellow out that memorable line, "A horse, a horse, my kingdom for a horse." When the whole audience exploded in laughter, we wondered what had happened. The next morning's paper carried the story of how one hefty black and white tomcat had meowed across the stage right at the verbal cue. It turned out that it was our own cat, Sylvester, out on the prowl. Life was cuddly and comfortable, filled with simple reliable pleasures.

During the day when friends would stop by and ask why I was hunched over a microphone talking to my tape deck, I confessed what I was considering. "Are you crazy?" several asked. "Think of all the competition." One friend remarked, "Think of all the young beauties with journalism degrees from posh schools whose parents know all the right people!"

Of course, they were right, but I had already considered those things before deciding I really had nothing to lose. By that time, I was already choosing which of the two local TV stations I would first approach in my attempt to get a foot in the broadcast door.

KMST, the CBS affiliate in nearby Monterey, was where I went first. I told the personnel director I had a bachelor's degree, a nose for news, and a determination to see if I could do it well. I showed her writing samples and offered to make an audition tape. As it turned out, they were looking for a female anchorwoman who would also shoot, write, edit, and report. They asked me to audition for that spot.

And so came my very first time on camera. There was, from the beginning, a rush of excitement in delivering both myself and my information into the unblinking eye. My long beach-bleached hair was swept up into the so-called French roll.

Lorenzo had bought me a new blazer and pretty silk blouse, which I wore with his good wishes. I found that as they rolled the tape, my heart did seem to beat a little faster, the voice edge a little higher with anticipation, and the perspiration flow more freely under the intensity of the studio wattage. I was enchanted by all of it. I saw that it was clearly not going to be easy to do this well. It would take a great deal of practice to imbue the on-camera work with the same sort of composure one achieved when constructing the stories off the air. Despite my novice state, I couldn't fail to notice that this was the first thing other than surfing that had so totally captured my interest. I was acquiring a new addiction, filled with all kinds of diverse promise. It was a career which would finally allow me to make use of my knowledge and love of language.

But my first audition did not result in the job I hoped for. My path wasn't going to be quite that easy. They gave the anchor spot to someone with more on-air experience, as they should have. But they didn't just dismiss me; they asked if I would like to do some commercial spots for a local car dealer, just to get started.

Soon my first paid TV job had me pitching Chevrolets. "When I buy a car, I'm cautious, careful, and very concerned about my investment. That's why Prolo Chevrolet in Santa Cruz gets my business." Then I smiled brightly as little cars whizzed across my teeth. This was due to a defect of a low-budget chroma-key system which projected mistakenly on to my enamel as well as on to the screen behind me. The engineers never seemed to fix the problem completely and every time I'd see those commercials, the cars would be there, moving inside my mouth.

Undaunted and thirty-five dollars richer, my next stop was the NBC affiliate in neighboring Salinas, the nation's lettuce bowl. "I want to be a reporter," I told the production manager. "That's nice," he said, "but we need someone to do the weather. Come back and audition tomorrow."

That evening I installed myself in the stacks of the Carmel

Public Library. I knew little more than the average citizen about weather and weather forecasting. Surfers tend to be aware of low-pressure systems because such phenomena generate wave action. But I had barely a clue about how to prepare for the next day's audition. Geography seemed a good place to start. I relearned the location of all the states. Lorenzo quizzed me relentlessly, "North Dakota, South Dakota," until the map of the U.S. was branded into my brain. Then I moved on to books on weather fundamentals.

It became apparent very quickly that weather forecasting is an inexact science. In essence, "prediction" is exactly that. The National Weather Service provides broadcasters with daily summaries of what has already happened. As to what will happen, the percentages of accuracy plunge after the first six hours. Television stations usually include the weather segment as a grace note on newscasts. It is an excellent way for a new on-air person to break in, because one must become adept at ad-libbing. Since there is no script, the weather person has to be relaxed and conversational without a teleprompter and with nothing more than the maps and symbols to serve as guidelines.

The next day I was put to the test. I must have passed, because they hired me to do the weeknight weathercasts live at six and eleven. I had finally gotten a foothold. I would be paid a weekly salary of seventy-five dollars. Thrilled to be hired and willing to do what they asked, I cut the sun-streaked mane to just an inch above my shoulders. Mother dear lent me her Saks charge card for some new outfits. The station gave me a portable weather radio and I started to learn.

It was great fun to be a weathergirl. You could be creative with the limited material in a way that other on-air people could not be. But after just two weeks, I was champing at the bit to be more than the loquacious cutie standing next to the stationary front. I hinted heavily to the news director how smart it would be for him to let me go shoot a story. He finally relented in response to my repeated requests and placed a CP-16 film camera in my waiting arms.

"There's a body reported on some guy's lawn three blocks from here; the story is yours. Get going!"

Racing to the scene I saw that there was indeed a body on a lawn. With the cumbersome and weighty CP on my right shoulder, the microphone in my left hand, I took some wide shots of the neighbors gawking at a prone, white-draped figure surrounded by policemen. That done, I dashed up to the officer in charge and rolled the film while he answered my questions about what had happened. The man under wraps had done himself in. Since suicides aren't covered in newscasts, I knew that my footage would not be used. But I was anxious to get back to the station and see how it had turned out anyway.

The two-hour wait for the processing chemicals seemed interminable. But when my film finally emerged from the soup, the first appraisal was good. At the very least, I had recorded an image. Mounting the footage on an edit reel, I rolled through the first fifty feet, smiling at what was lurching across the viewing screen. The wide shots of the scene were effective, in focus, and correctly exposed, even if a little shaky. True, some of the shots seemed a little different from what I thought I had shot. Then came the interview portion and a surreal surprise! Mistaking the parameters of the viewfinder, I had managed to capture the policeman only from the nose down. There he was, very lucid in his explanation of why there was a body on the lawn. His lips were flapping, his nostrils flaring. Instantly I understood the vagaries of the viewfinder margins on that camera, just as my newsroom colleagues snorted good-naturedly about my pig-snout technique.

Another learning experience came during a merciless heat wave that hit the Salinas Valley in the summer of 1974. The general manager marched into the studio one day when I was preparing for the six o'clock weather forecast. Actually I smelled him coming. He was short and heavy, a chain smoker preferring very long, fat cigars. Wearing his trademark blanket plaid jacket, coiffed with a blondined pompadour, and bejeweled with a diamond horseshoe pinky ring, he had a request.

"Christine," he said to me, "This heat spell really has the farmers worried about their crops. I'd like you to cheer them up by doing the weather in your bikini tomorrow."

This request was followed by billows of cigar smoke which I'm sure obscured my reaction. I was too numb to do much more than nod in muted accord.

How was I going to deal with this? The next day I arrived at work in a trenchcoat buttoned up tightly at the neck. My floor director asked what on earth I had up my sleeve. I assured him that he need not worry about anything other than cueing me through the weather as he was used to doing every day.

When the moment of truth arrived and the anchorman pitched my segment, I looked into the live camera and said, still in my trenchcoat, "During this heat spell people, mostly men, have been asking me to do the weather in my bathing suit. I've been too shy to do it, up until now. But tonight, I've finally worked up the courage, and I'm going to do the weather in my bathing suit."

Pausing for a few beats, I then opened the trench to reveal... a turn-of-the-century rented bathing costume complete with ruffles, bloomers, bags, bows, the world's most unattractive swim garb. That done, I proceeded to give the weather information with a perfectly straight face and demeanor. Everyone, especially the general manager, seemed to get a kick out of it. For years after that I believed the best way to deal with sexism was with humor. I was not by nature a litigious person.

From that point on, I was given more responsibilities at the station. I could shoot, edit and report local news events. Once a week I produced and anchored "Capitol Report," a segment on how Sacramento legislation affected our community. I became the station's public service director and booth announcer as well. When the regular sports anchor took a long vacation, I was asked to do sportscasts. Since I had grown up in a household where my father was a football and basketball coach, I had more awareness of sports and sports trivia than most women. Actually, my year and a half in Salinas was on-the-job training in the nation's ninety-eighth market and I loved every minute of it.

Yet I was becoming complacent. I had no burning ambitions or even casual thoughts about better-paying jobs in larger markets. But as the result of circumstances and luck, more than intent, I was to find myself out of my marriage into a series of relationships that were both destructive and productive, and into a much better job.

It started innocently enough. One day in the Salinas newsroom, I read the wire reports of a powerful hurricane headed for the population areas of Mazatlan, Mexico. It was predicted to hit land a few hours before airtime. I was concerned that I couldn't seem to nail down any information. Many of our viewers in Salinas were Latinos with relatives and friends living in Mazatlan. This was an important weather story and nobody seemed to know what was happening, not the weather service, nor anyone else. I guessed that probably the larger stations in San Francisco would have a better idea of the storm's progress, but I also didn't know if any of the big city weathermen would be approachable. Since we watched all the City stations in Carmel, I decided that at least one person, Joel Bartlett of the CBS station KPIX, would not be too aloof to help me out. When I called, he commiserated that his data were also sparse. We exchanged what little we knew and then he suggested that if I were to come up to San Francisco, he would be glad to show me the equipment used in the nation's sixth largest market.

It was an invitation I took up about three months later. One day I just hopped into my Volkswagen and drove up the coast, bringing a tape of reporting, sports and weather work.

When I arrived at the station, Joel Bartlett bounded down the steps to greet me. He was full of enthusiasm and good humor as he showed me around and told me about the production values at KPIX. In the midst of this, he casually said, "Did you know they're looking for someone to do weekend weather?"

I blurted out, "You've got to be kidding!" He asked me to follow him to the newsroom.

There he introduced me to Joe Russin, the news director and an atypical TV man. Russin had come straight from public television, San Francisco's KQED. The news programming there provided in-depth discussion of local issues. Reporters were free to grill each other live, on the air, without rehearsing the answers ahead of time. "Newsroom" was a reporter's broadcast. Coming from that background, Russin's ethics were contrary to those who would commercialize news, those who would call it a "product." He was not to last long working for Westinghouse, the owners of KPIX. Ironically, sound news decisions made during his tenure ultimately lifted the KPIX news rating up to first place in a highly competitive market. At the time I met him, he had a reputation of being both demanding and keen-minded. He was also an alleged womanizer, according to an article in *New West* magazine. Soon I was seated before him in a naugahyde lounge chair.

"Let me see the tape," he grunted, barely civil. As it rolled before our eyes, he grunted a few more times, stopping the tape at one point to say, "You look like last year's anchorwoman with that neck scarf."

He restarted the tape just as I began to slink down into the clinging recesses of the warm naugahyde. I hadn't wanted to be put in this position. I wasn't looking for another job. I was happy where I was. I kept telling myself these things as Russin sneered through the rest of my tape, finally stopping it and spinning around to face me. As I waited for some summary statement of dismissal, he surprised me. "You know you're very good, don't you?"

It was more of a challenge than a statement. Then before I could respond, Russin offered me a job. I'd do weather on the weekends and some reporting during the week. I'd have to sign a one-year contract.

I didn't even have to think about it. All my instincts were telling me I needed to be in San Francisco. I was ready for the next set of creative challenges, for new levels of professionalism. I had all kinds of ambition after all, hidden under a deceptively laid-back demeanor. It just took San Francisco and its exotic pulse to shake me out of my complacency.

FOR A COUPLE of months I commuted from Carmel to San Francisco on the weekends, still living with Lorenzo during the week. Then I met someone who overwhelmed me. A musician-artist, rock and roller, big city sophisticate—I was enchanted. And though I could see the notches on the bedpost that everyone else warned me about, I didn't care. This was one love rush that had to be experienced.

Since Lorenzo and I were such pals and had agreed never to lie to each other, I told him what had happened and we separated. Lorenzo needed now to be in Hollywood to pursue his editing and directing career. We both recognized the natural parting of our paths. Division of community property was pretty weird, though. He wound up getting custody of our two black and white cats, Sylvester and Bloom. We agreed that you shouldn't split up a good pair of cats. Cheeks full of tears, I drove away leaving a sweet chunk of my life behind. It would be a long time before I felt as pampered as I had felt, there in our Carmel cottage.

Sweeping into the vortex of high energy city life didn't allow a lot of time for reflection on my version of paradise lost. On the job they kept my tail hopping. My new lover was soon an ex-lover, the kind of person who gets a charge out of seducing someone away from common sense, but then has little interest when the love object is suddenly very much available.

The newscasts I was assigned to in San Francisco were on Saturdays and Sundays. I worked with two very hot men, both black, one on news, the other on sports. We used to joke that I was the "creme filling in the oreo cookie," or the white girl on "nigger news." The anchor, Andrew Hill, was quite erudite. He had written prize-winning interviews for major publications. He had a rich and reflective life outside of being a TV newsman. He was always impeccably dressed and always concerned about the content of the newscasts we presented. It was great to work with such a professional. Later Andrew was to resign from his prestigious and high-paying anchorman niche, something most people rarely do voluntarily. He had a powerful and well-reasoned dispute with the station over news coverage of the Bakke decision. That was the court ruling that determined that a white medical student had been the victim of "reverse discrimination." As a sensitive, black male journalist, Andrew saw the decision as a clear negative milestone for affirmative action. More importantly, Hill just couldn't be the on-camera mouthpiece for a newsroom that handled the Bakke case superficially, ignoring its far-reaching repercussions. After his resignation, he became a freelance writer and moved to Mendocino.

Jan Hutchins, the very hip, very cute, very counter-culture sport anchor, filled out our weekend team. Hutchins was and is a great flirt. He was fun to flirt back with. He's a clown, a guy with lots of genuine charisma. His charisma translated so well on camera that he was deemed the number two favorite sportscaster in the Bay Area, and he only worked two days a week! Coupled with these winners, I had high hopes for improvement.

One evening Andrew told me to put a smile on my face. The ratings books for the first period I had been on the newscast showed a solid two-point upswing. That small success urged me to become more aggressive in asking the news director to let me do more than the weather. I started out doing the lighter pieces: a women's sailing regatta, prepunkers in the *Rocky Horror Picture Show* cult at the Powell Street Cinema. Little by little I got to do more stories with an edge to them: an Oakland karate class for rape victims, the emergence of gay political power in San Francisco and its chief spokesman Harvey Milk, a series on Methadone clinics in the South Bay. But just as I was really getting into a reportorial role and roll, I blew a big story, totally blew it! It wound up costing me much momentum, three steps back and none ahead.

The story Joe Russin assigned me to cover was that of Inez Garcia, a beautiful Latina woman who killed the man who held her down during a brutal rape. She then had been convicted of murder under much controversy, and had already served nineteen months of a prison term. A savvy Berkeley woman lawyer, Susan Jordan, got her a new trial on procedural grounds.

Joe Russin decided to take a chance with me. I was familiar with the Salinas area where the trial was being held. I was certainly earnest enough, and he felt that the earlier pieces I had done held some promise.

The logistics of covering this trial in a town two and a half a half hours away by car from San Francisco were very specific. I would hire a local cameraman to shoot my stories. Then, if the story warranted it, a helicopter would pick up our sealed film cans for delivery to the film lab at KPIX. This was news gathering at its most expensive. There was immense pressure on me to succeed.

Terrific luck greeted our first day of covering the story. I had hired the son of my old Salinas cameraman. He and his father had just acquired a new CP-16 film camera. After sitting all morning in the courtroom getting the gist of things, as the defense rested its case and the jury was sent out, we went to lunch at Rose's Cantina. Inez Garcia, out on bail, also had chosen to eat there. We talked with her for an hour off-camera over mutual plates of tortillas, beans, and rice. I heard firsthand her description of what had happened. In the macho world of barrio drug-dealing where women dared not speak out, Inez Garcia had defied every taboo. When her assailant threatened to stab her son if she spoke out, Garcia became a warrior and killed, she said, in self-defense. The case and retrial with the brilliant feminist lawyer had become a *cause célèbre*. Inez was aware of all the support in the packed courtroom.

My cameraman and I worked on our story, shooting our stand-ups in front of the theater one block from the courthouse. On the marquee the movie *Lipstick*—a rape-revenge thriller—played in town by coincidence.

When we finished doing the voice-over tracks and getting our extra shots, we waited at the Salinas airport for the copter to land and take our package and script. Not even shutting off his engines, he whisked down and then swooped away. I waited anxiously to hear how our offerings had been received. Two and a half hours later we heard that there had been no image and no sound on our film. After all the expense, all the effort, the god-damned drama of the whirlybird, and a really worthwhile story, it had been lost forever to some evil genie. "See, I told you so's" came from the naysayers at the station who had questioned Russin's trust in someone so green. My poor cameraman, knowing that his lack of performance had really set me back, didn't quite know what had gone wrong. Then he discovered that the brand-new camera, unlike the old one he'd been used to, had a different battery warning system. It was a mortifying error. I managed to do a phone interview from the scene when the Garcia acquittal came down. I also salvaged a report that was used by the CBS radio network. But the major emotion in all of this was one of "You should've seen the one that got away."

After that unlucky day, I was given more sports than news assignments. I tried to make the most of these as well as the opportunities to anchor the sportscasts when both of the two male anchors were away. This situation gave me some big-market basic training under a good sports producer who helped me get by with what I didn't know. KPIX gave me a chance to improve my voice-over play-by-plays until I actually enjoyed doing them.

Reporting on the U.S. Open Championships and writing my copy from CBS radio, I also made at least one major painful blunder. I blithely went on the air and told viewers who had just won. I wasn't cognizant of the fact that my own network was set to rebroadcast the match via tape delay right after our newscast.

Regardless of that gaffe, when CBS Sports was scouting the country for a woman sportscaster, I was one of six women they asked to audition. The network had requested its affiliates to send tapes of any promising female sportscasters. KPIX complied and soon I was in a taxi bound for West 57th Street and a tryout at CBS Sports.

It went well. I felt very relaxed, as if I had nothing to lose. Unlike most auditions, this one included the presentation of your own three-minute commentary on why CBS should specifically give more coverage to women's athletics. I felt that was the strongest part of my bid for this new job. When I finished, I flew right back to San Francisco to do my own newscasts that same evening. Despite an exhausting day, I felt energetic. It wasn't so much because I thought I would get the network job, but because I knew I had given my best effort.

CBS was looking for a host for a newly-conceived "Women in Sports" segment for the CBS Sports Spectacular. Rather than a Miss America or an athlete's pretty wife, they said they were looking for a "meat and potatoes" sports journalist. They had been attracted to the tapes of sports pieces I had done in San Francisco. They also expressed interest in my production and writing abilities, as well as my "natural good looks." They called two weeks after the audition to tell me I had a new job. After only two-and-a-half years of television news experience, I was going to a network. Admittedly I'd be but a small minnow in the biggest and classiest pond, but I'd be swimming nonetheless.

The job itself seemed tailor-made; to host the live segment every Saturday on "Sports Spectacular" out of New York, exchanging patter with the male host, Pat Summerall, Tom Brookshier, or Brent Musberger. The four remaining minutes of the segment would be allotted to a pretaped profile of a woman athlete, from various sports. Each week we would fly to a different part of the country with a production team to do our stories whererever they cropped up. The travel, the chance to meet world-class competitors in their own environments, the prestige of having a role on a live network program, all of it seemed great. Then they offered to upgrade my "California" image.

Figuring that they knew what they were doing, I gave CBS Sports carte blanche to do with me what they would. Soon I sat caped in a chic East Fifties beauty salon with over one hundred silver foil antennae jutting from my scalp. Chemical glop oozed down the back of my ear adding yet another sensation to a very bizarre experience. My senses heightened once again when wedgie cutouts were positioned over each of my slightly wild eyebrows to dye them black. "So much better on camera," I was told. When they finished with me, I emerged into a beautiful New York City snowstorm with a platinum blond Dorothy Hammill wedge cut, black eyebrows and dark red lips. Wearing a full-length borrowed sheepskin coat, I trudged back to my hotel through the cold clean air. I caught sight of my reflection in a shop window. Who the hell was I supposed to be?

Later that night, coming into San Francisco on the red-eye flight, I was picked up at the airport by friends who didn't even recognize me. "I can't stand that kind of hair cut," dared one pal who knew I couldn't either. "It'll grow out," volunteered another. "That's just what I'm afraid of," I told them both. My normally brownish-reddish dark blonde hair grew rapidly. I didn't want this to be the network premiere of "Roots."

My debut was just a week away when another modification of my appearance took place. While playing a speedy game of racquetball at a San Francisco health club, I was sideswiped on the temple by my partner's racquet edge. A large blue bump bulged from my forehead. Boy, was I glad it hadn't hit my eye! But in a mere hour, the swelling had invaded the eye socket. By week's end the eye was purple, mauve, yellow and green, a true challenge for the makeup artists at CBS. They did their best, I went on the air and the first thing host Tom Brooksheir said to me was, "I see you've got a real mouse on that eye." I replied to the best of my ability, "But Tom, you'd never know it, thanks to the miracles of modern cosmetology."

Even after the eye was well-healed, I always felt uncomfortable in the image the beauticians had created. I learned at least how important it was for me to feel natural and uncontrived. I didn't mind a little artifice as long as it wasn't glaring. But when it was overdone, I couldn't help but balk.

It was disconcerting, too, that at the network level, "talent" was frequently told what to say and in what sequence to say it. In many ways, it wasn't nearly as much fun as the hands-on approach in small television markets.

I also learned that my best abilities as a broadcaster stemmed from my being pretty much the same on the air as I am in person. Women's and men's magazines make much over "make-overs," as if most people are dissatisfied with what they look like. Being "made-over" has become akin to being "born-again," a necessary rite of passage for anyone upward-bound. I clearly was of a different persuasion.

With all of those lessons included, the CBS experience was basically terrific, even though it didn't garner much success. Cancelled after nine months and three option renewals, "Women in Sports" went virtually unheralded. For what I learned about myself, my strengths and weaknesses, and for all the places CBS sent me, I felt nonetheless most appreciative. I experienced the terrifying excitement of watching a woman bullfighter nearly gored in a small corrida a few hours outside of Mexico City. From a converted DC-2 we eyeballed the American Women's Skydiving team as it formed a perfect star above the Arizona desert. "Women in Sports" interviewed Evonne Goolagong, a mistress of the stringed instrument. We talked to American track queens Decker, Frederick, and Tyus. California's motorcross queen Cherry Stockton instructed me in basic 250cc riding. I got to run in the redwoods with a seventy-one-year-old woman marathoner, Mavis Lindgren. We covered women's collegiate rodeo near Billings, Montana, and the Mayflower Golf Classic as Nancy Lopez eagled her way to another tour victory in Indianapolis.

When the show's option wasn't picked up again, CBS asked me to co-host the World Professional Speed Skateboard Championships. Now the kind of skateboarding done in empty swimming pools, huge dry concrete drainage pipes, and skateparks is exciting to show on videotape with music, but this particular event was basically just downhill racing, probably the most impossible event to have to comment upon. Skateboarding gladiators race wheel-to-wheel down the incline at Derby Downs in Akron, Ohio, the home of the soapbox derby.

Rain delayed our taping for four days, and so meeting the best skateboarders in the world meant getting some new friends. Along with them, I discovered that Akron has some of the best tiered parking garages in the midwest. Impervious to the rain, we set up an obstacle course in an unfinished garage and whiled away the hours cranking hard turns on virgin cement.

After the rains cleared, we shot the show. My swan song at CBS entailed announcing a very boring skateboard race: "Look at that, look verrry closely, he's pulling ahead by a ball bearing!" That was the end of my stint at CBS. I was a California woman headed home and back to her real roots, which wouldn't have to be platinum anymore.

Back in San Francisco briefly, I converted a friend's unused auto body shop into an art gallery. I presented a show of the sculpture and paintings of Paul Lindhard, an artist and dear friend I had known since college. One of San Francisco's finest gallery owners took a liking to Paul's work and took on five of the sculptures. Selling art is hard but exciting work, probably much harder than TV News. The show was a nice goodbye to San Francisco.

With several of my closest friends conspiring to bring me back to Santa Barbara, it was an easy move to make.

The one television station in town has probably the prettiest location of any TV station in the country, KEYT, the ABC affiliate in Santa Barbara, sits on top of a prominent hill across from a beautiful coastal mountain range. Beneath and to the east lies the quasi-Spanish splendor of Santa Barbara, an endless sea of red-tiled roofs and glistening fountains. Sweeping out to the west the view encompasses harbor and marina, the expanse of ocean and the Channel Islands.

In market size placed at 116th, this was a station where reporters were camerapeople, editors, anchors, and anything else that was needed. Though a union shop, the station was small enough so that news employees were allowed to use equipment and thus to have that hands-on situation that I had so enjoyed in the past.

Here, as had been the case before in both Salinas and San Francisco, I was doing weather, sports, and news. I also co-anchored the nightly eleven o'clock newscasts. My co-anchor could not have been more unlike me, his right-wing fundamentalism clashed with my liberal beliefs. Surprisingly, this conflict worked to our advantage, making us a team. We had the choice of fighting like cats and dogs or reaching some degree of consensus and compromise. In a classic example of role reversal, by the time we had anchored together for a year-and-a-half, we were both very different people. We had been forced to absorb each other's ideas and became friends in the process.

I was not at all interested in anchoring in a larger market. My career had been both diversified and fulfilling up to this point. I had a strong sense of self, in both my victories and failures. In addition, I had always loved the Santa Barbara community and had become involved in public service activities, often spending personal time in oil hearings, planning commission sessions, or at trials. My interest was genuine and uncontrived. Even though the Santa Barbara salary was only $20,000 per year, I was not looking for the bigger paycheck or the wider audience. I was content to be in a place where the emphasis was on getting the stories and getting them right. Only once did management mention my appearance, and that was telling me that I needed to pull my hair back a bit. Shooting, editing, producing, writing, and anchoring, I felt I was doing some of the best work of my television career.

Then one day I got an unsolicited phone call that would change my life. "Christine, line two. It's long distance from Kansas City."

2.

KANSAS CITY, nice town with nice people, I thought when I heard the name. Though I had no first-hand knowledge of the place, it did have a pleasantly bland image in the lexicon of American placenames.

"This is Ridge Shannon," the Kansas City caller identified himself. "I'm news director here at KMBC, the ABC affiiliate."

His name sounded like a put-on, but who was I to question, with my own nautical, albeit authentic, sobriquet—Chris Craft (just like the boat).

"That's nice," I answered. Then he launched into superlatives about a tape he'd just seen of my anchor work. It was possible, he said, that I was just the person they were looking for in a female nightly anchor at six and ten. This would be the first they'd made such an opportunity for a woman. He said they were looking to "join the modern age" like the other stations in town which already had the male/female co-anchor format.

"Mr. Shannon, I'm flattered that you like a tape you've seen, but I also must question where you acquired it since I am not looking for another job."

He answered that the tape had been provided by a Dallas-based consulting firm that was helping them find anchor candidates. These people known as The Media Associates had set up their gear in hotel rooms in different cities and made dubs of local newscasters without their permission.

Reiterating to him that I was not looking to leave Santa Barbara, I also was frank with him on another subject. Ridge Shannon was to hear my admonition more than once: "I am a thirty-six-year-old woman with lines, bags, wrinkles, the signs of my experience. I am not a fixture, a beauty queen, or a token." I also let him know that I had been a surfer and ocean lover for many years and that I had "probably seen too much sun, and would continue to do so."

During that first phone call and and in every subsequent one between Kansas City and Santa Barbara, I repeated to Ridge Shannon ad nauseum that appearance simply was not my top priority. I was primarily interested in working in a newsroom where getting the stories and getting them right was the top criterion. Perhaps I was naive in hoping that such a TV newsroom could exist in this day and age, but I was adamant about those basic standards. I told him of my experience at CBS and what it had taught me about myself. Again and again I told him that what he saw was what he got. In return, he professed total understanding.

In that first conversation, I conceded that I hadn't ruled out opportunities that happened to come my way. Actually, I'd often thought that the ideal career for a television reporter would include stints in each of the major regions of the country. Any writer or journalist appreciates the value of an informed overview. The job of news anchoring also exposes you to a variety of social and political opportunities. It certainly didn't seem like a bad way to get an overview of the Midwest, in short order. Such a situation could be a crash course in the history, customs, progress, decay, politics, and people of the nation's center. Motion picture companies, after all, very often test-market their new movies in Kansas City. It's supposed to be a bellweather of centrist opinion. Any journalist worth his or her salt could not fail to see the value of tapping the sources and dimensions of such opinion. I did not automatically rule out Ridge Shannon's inquiries. Professionally, it's a good idea to audition for a job if you are asked to. It can be a good test of your skills and mettle, even if you are not overwhelmed by the prospective job.

Some of my Santa Barbara friends thought I was a glutton

for punishment. But the more I considered Ridge Shannon's continued phone calls, it seemed harmless enough to fly back for an audition. I had a mild but genuine curiosity about a place that had nothing in common with Santa Barbara.

"A surfer in Kansas City?" asked one friend. "You'll go berserk, that's cruel and inhuman punishment, much like a fish out of water!" opined another. Of course I knew that if I ended up actually moving there, my aquatic pursuits would be greatly curtailed. I also knew that Santa Barbara would still be my home.

What vaguely disturbed me more than the locale was the fact that KMBC was owned by broadcast conglomerate giant Metromedia. Most of their television stations across the country were independents, not affiliated with any network. KMBC happened to be an ABC affiliate, which bespoke of hopefully better national news feed than at the independents.

But I had heard a very unsettling comment about Metromedia at one of their stations, about a year before the Kansas City inquiry.

At the Washington, D.C., station, WTTG, they had been looking for a woman to do dual duty as a sportscaster and reporter. They had contacted me right after I left CBS and I had flown back to audition for them, putting together a story and doing a sports anchor test. The male anchor stopped me as I came down a hallway between newsroom and studio and issued me a clandestine warning, "Don't ever work for Metromedia, they are cheap bastards!" I thought his remark was curious. When I heard later that he was in his last week at the station, I rationalized that his caveat was merely the traditional parting shot.

The phone calls kept coming from Kansas City to Santa Barbara. A dear friend, Bob Hamilton, offered to act as an intermediary in talking to Metromedia on my behalf. Bob had been a contract lawyer at one time for Universal Studios, then he had gone on to a very successful career as a writer and producer of television movies, action series, and particularly miniseries. A year younger, Bob lived in a two-story Spanish beach house on one of the most beautiful private coves in Santa Barbara. We knew each other from mutual torture sessions at the local Nautilus facility. Fun at the gym and gracious too about public access, he always let me go surfing at his beach. Consistent with his basically generous nature, Bob offered to help me with the Kansas City people without reimbursement.

One morning we were basking in the indolent sunlight on his bougainvillea-draped front deck. I was reading some of his "Magnum P.I." scripts and he was scoping out the Wall Street Journal. Next to us were large crystal tumblers of fresh-squeezed orange juice, thick with nutritious pulp. The telephone cord stretched from the house to the phone just next to Bob's chaise. A call came, and not answering on the first ring but the third, Bob's face soon switched from relaxed to intent. I could hear everything he was saying, "Yes, Ridge, I know that Metromedia says it won't deal with agents or representatives, but Christine has asked me to help assure her that the details of any dealings between the two of you remain clearly defined."

Bob then launched into a vivid reiteration of my attitudes regarding personal appearance and changes thereto. This included a reprise of the CBS experience. Bob emphasized to Ridge several times that I had to be an anchor who also got to go out in the field. Ridge replied that he and the general manager, R. Kent Replogle, both agreed they liked what they saw and wouldn't want to change a thing. Would I come back to Kansas City for that audition? Under those representations, I would and did.

Ridge Shannon and I met face to face for the first time at the Kansas City airport. He wore his hair in the type of crewcut usually given to gradeschool boys in rural neighborhoods. A puckish face gone to middle age was accented by glasses. He was rather lean, priding himself on running minimarathons. As he talked about his running, I was distracted to see enthusiastic collections of spittle form at both corners of his mouth. Later I discovered that staying out of the line of fire was to be a frequent challenge when talking to Ridge.

For our first meeting, I happened to be wearing sporty pants and a velour top. I was certainly not trying to dazzle him with my attire. On the contrary, I saw no reason to dress for travel any differently than I ever did. I was unwilling to add to the discomfort of airplanes by wearing uncomfortable and restricting garments. I remember too that I happened to be wearing an aging pair of cowboy boots, about the only thing (other than running shoes) that I could wear for any length of time. A painful bone deformation of both feet runs in the matrilineal side of my family. I had been through two unsuccessful foot surgeries and was not able to find much in the way of elegant footwear.

As a response to his nervously checking out my extremities, I looked him square in the eye and told him of this problem and of a compromise I had reached regarding television. If called upon to sit on an open set, I would wear low-heeled pumps for those wide shots. I could not, however, walk in the kind of stiletto heeled, cramped toe, bondage shoes that many women apparently endure because they think men find them sexually exciting. I understood the erotic allure of pretty shoes and occasionally envied women who could wear them with comfort, but I was clearly not one of their number.

Ridge said he understood perfectly, "Why we never see your feet anyway! What difference could that make?"

What difference indeed! We embarked on a tour of Kansas City and its more attractive environs. Ridge abruptly dismissed the rotting downtown area and made certain that I saw Country Club Plaza. It was ersatz Spanish, new and charming with Tiffany, Gucci, and Brooks Brothers outlets. You'd have no trouble buying a Rolex here.

Most of what I saw certainly seemed sufficiently up to date. Kansas Citians, for the most part, spend an awful lot of time assuring visitors just how contemporary they are. They really don't need to. The very provinciality they dread is probably their greatest charm.

As we drove past golf courses, private clubs, and suburban homes, I was getting a better feel for the place. The massive Nelson Art Gallery with its bronze Henry Moore sheep on the lawn was the most impressive sight. Loose Park where Christo had done his "Wrapped Sidewalks" was glistening in a light snow. Reflecting the prisms of winter light, Dale Eldred's Brush Creek panel assemblage was quite simply dazzling. For its size, Kansas City seemed to have a lot of interesting art. In fact, this Midwestern city has more fountains than any other American city. And the fountains themselves are very often sculpturally sophisticated.

Kansas City seemed civilized and attractive enough. Ridge pointed out the sights while he pitched some pertinent selling points about the TV station.

He described how KMBC had state-of-the-art microwave equipment featuring two live-capability trucks that we used nearly every night for the newscasts. Broadcasting live from the scene of a breaking news event is one of the most challenging things done in local television news. Since my stint in San Francisco years before, I hadn't had the opportunity to do unscripted live shots. Small stations like the one in Santa Barbara still don't have the in-house technology for frequent live shots. Sometimes they rent the needed equipment for elections, but that is only a rare opportunity. However, medium market and large-market television stations must have the electronic capability to stay competitive.

Ridge's idea was to have the co-anchors take turns out in the field whenever there was a big story that was appropriate for a live shot. That concept was one of the major inducements that caught my attention as he continued his praise of KMBC and his derision of the two other major competitors in town.

KCMO (CBS) had a young pretty model anchorette, Anne Peterson, who was coupled with the deep-throated perennial favorite, Wendell Anschutz. Anne was in her early twenties, genuinely sweet, "a real audience turn-on," said Ridge, "and an albatross around the neck of journalism." Apparently she had only the most limited reporting experience and a very hard time with interviews. The knowledgeable part of the team, Anshutz, was in his mid-forties with lines, wrinkles, and deep black bags under his eyes. He had a voice tinged with credibility and comfort. He didn't need to show an awful lot of intellectual initiative and he didn't. People liked him because he'd been around for a while. Other reporters respected him as a colleague and a very nice guy. KCMO had led in the ratings war for some three years prior to my arrival.

The NBC affiliate, WDAF, was dead last in ratings, but appealed to older Kansas Citians as the place they turned most frequently for news. An affable and zany weatherman and two anchors surnamed Smith led the roster there. Stacey Smith was benignly competent and Cynthia Smith had the local advantage of being a community activist. Her background included doing weather and selling TV time, but little reporting. I was to find Cynthia professional and genuinely concerned about what happened in Kansas City. Ridge thought she was "hard and brassy, not a good journalist." He was looking for a competent journalist with good credentials. He said he wanted a person with real substance, real credibility, someone who could be held accountable in the field. That is the benchmark. How well do you perform under fire? Ridge Shannon thought he wanted me.

But first there would be the test, an on-camera audition with the incumbent male anchor, Scott Feldman. It was set for the following day. Later in my hotel room with a cup of hot cocoa I watched the local newscasts on all three stations and then slept confidently. It was nice to be inside the Muehlbach Hotel, which had been a frequent resting place for President Harry Truman.

The next morning, I crunched through some fresh snow to the station, located downtown in the old Lyric Opera House building, a Kansas City landmark. My cheeks were teased red by the raw nip in the air. Ridge met me at the entrance and escorted me through the basement hallways and into the subterranean newsroom where I was introduced to reporters and staffers. Most of them did friendly double-takes when they got a load of my attire. I was wearing a pretty beige cashmere sweater, a thin gold chain with a simple ornament at the throat, black velveteen Calvin Klein pants and my western orthopedic clodhoppers. One of the staff members told me later that the two other auditionees had worn seamed nylons and what Shelley Winters has so eloquently referred to as "fuck-me" shoes.

The solo anchor, Scott Feldman, had been by himself for three years and, like anyone else in a similar position, was more than a bit reluctant to share the limelight. Since management had already decided he'd be paired with someone, his best bet was to have some input into the selection.

Scott was the kind of guy who had no cowlicks. St. Louis born, Jewish bred, he later told me he always adhered to a very wise saying of his father's: "When the going gets rough, just play dumb." Scott was both a good reporter and a news reader with a deep resonant voice. Handsome and telegenic, he was very much the ideal anchorman, and younger than I was. Supposedly, he could be a prima donna and yet could also work very hard.

I enjoyed doing the audition with Scott. Even though he could assume a chilly reserve if he felt the slightest bit threatened, he also had that healthy breed of sarcastic humor that is emblematic of newspeople. We took turns reading copy and then contrived an interview where Scott played the role of a newly elected senator and I, the interviewer. We had, at least in the audition, a conversational ease that came very naturally. When the audition was over, I felt I had done my best.

A solicitous Ridge Shannon ushered me up to the sixth floor executive suite. There I was introduced to the general manager, R. Kent Replogle, who had been watching the audition via closed circuit monitor in his offices. He was affable, very complimentary about what he had just seen, and offered his management perspective of both the Kansas City television market and the importance of his station's news efforts.

I could not help but notice Replogle's uncanny resemblance to the actor Roddy McDowell in full makeup for *Planet of the Apes*. In a way, it was reassuring to look at Replogle's decidedly simian features. Surely this man, who readily did on-camera editorials, could not have demanded cosmetic symmetry or perfectly tamed hair as a prerequisite for on-air spokespeople.

He asked me if I wanted the job. Mind you, this man was looking at me square in the face. He had seen me both in person and on tape. He was about to hear first-hand what was most important to me: getting out in the field and not having my appearance changed. He had no intention of changing my appearance, he said. He wanted me frequently out in the field to garner local credibility because he was impressed by my journalistic skills. As the interview continued, he described how the station employed consultants from Dallas. "They come in and give advice from time to time," he said. That certainly didn't sound too intrusive, I thought.

We agreed that I should look at a copy of the "standard Metromedia contract." We would talk further after I had gone back to Santa Barbara.

Ridge drove me back to the airport to catch my return flight. As we rode along, he waxed enthusiastic over my audition, and he sought out my attitudes on taking the co-anchor job. When we arrived, I had a half hour's wait at the airport, and Ridge wanted to continue our talk over beer. Getting more personal, he told me about his background and family. At one time, he had been a news director at a much larger station in Detroit, WXYZ, an ABC owned and operated affiliate. It hadn't worked out and he'd been fired. Before long, though, he landed himself a job in a smaller market where the climes were to prove more amenable to his style of operation. His family had found the new town, Kansas City, much to their liking and he was eager to continue pleasing Metromedia.

Ridge made much of other parts of his background including his years as a producer for the NBC station in Washington, D.C. He detailed an experience more befitting a newsman than a salesman. We agreed that all too many television news directors in this day and age are unfortunately mere flack catchers between sales departments and newsrooms. Even top network news chiefs often have negligible credentials in actually covering stories. Ridge's description of his own skills was certainly an inducement for me to give this job offer more serious consideration.

Loosened by the beer, Ridge began asking me questions about my personal life. I mentioned my marital separation and told him that it was not particularly regrettable. He asked me about personal habits. Did I smoke marijuana? I told him that I had tried it but found it overrated. He "confided" in me that he'd always wanted to try it, but that he feared what his wife and daughters would think if they ever found out. The announcement of my plane's departure mercifully ended this conversation. We exchanged farewells and I left.

During the following week there were several more phone calls to Santa Barbara, all placed by Metromedia. In each of those calls, Bob Hamilton or I reiterated my two chief concerns: no change of appearance and opportunities to go in the field. Each time those issues were raised, Metromedia agreed that they wanted me to do frequent reporting and frequent live shots. I remember Bob's unveiled admonition, "Christine is not a beauty queen; she's an aging California surfer who just happens to be a bright journalist. She's probably seen too much sun. She is a 'natural' with little artifice, preferring to direct her energies to more professional priorities." He was being candid, to be sure, but neither Bob nor I wanted any lack of understanding on the points at hand.

When salary negotiations began, Metromedia made its first

offer to me, a whopping $28,000, only $8,000 more than I was making in Santa Barbara, and in no way a sufficient financial inducement to leave paradise. Going from the 116th market to the 27th in the country, one could at least legitimately expect a doubling of salary. We countered with $40,000. Had we known Scott Feldman's earnings, we would have gone higher. Feldman was then making $52,000 per year and was about to go up to $75,000 during the same period I was drawing $35,000, the figure we eventually settled on. In my experience and in the experience of others, salary differentials for the same job bore no relation to Equal Pay Act standards at Metromedia's newsroom in Kansas City. That was a fact that would be unveiled in courtroom proceedings nearly three years later.

But for the time being, I accepted Messrs. Shannon and Replogle pretty much at their word. I would never have left Santa Barbara had I known how coy they really were.

I made one additional trip back to Kansas City to find a place to live, selecting an inexpensive apartment, the third floor of a big older house in a neighborhood bustling with a renaissance. A fresh coat of snow blanketed the place, giving it a homey Currier and Ives appearance.

Back in Santa Barbara, as I tied up loose ends and helped the mover put my things in a van, Ridge phoned from Kansas City and asked me to do him a little favor. "We'd like you to stop by our consultants in Dallas on your way in, just to get to know them and see some of the services they can offer you." I agreed, seeing no harm in just stopping by on the way. "You'll be meeting Lynn Wilford. The two of you can have lunch and spend some time looking at the facilities there. I think you'll like Lynn. She's bright and energetic. She is one of Media Associates' key people. She can be very helpful to you."

It was a cold and unpleasant drizzly Dallas morning when I finally met Lynn Wilford on her own Texas turf. We exchanged pleasantries. She was the embodiment of the career gal image as expressed so relentlessly by magazines like

Glamour, Mademoiselle, and *Cosmopolitan.* Slender, chic, with just the right jewelry and not too much makeup, Lynn was quite attractive. She told me about her background for news consulting. She had been a drama major at the University of Texas, doing several plays while in college. She made no claim to having worked in a newsroom, or having been a reporter. She told me how some stations had asked her to be their anchor. She acknowledged it was because she so looked the part. Every stickpin, every bowed blouse had the right style of "credibility."

She was a walking encyclopedia of how colors and textures and fabrics can be used to enhance an anchor's impact on the community. I was amused by the depths of her expertise, but not too alarmed. After all, Ridge had assured me she only gave advice from time to time. Lynn put it this way, "My suggestions to you can be used to embellish your already established ability!" Never did she hint at the true nature of what her power would be to order my life at Metromedia.

As if she were letting me in on a big secret, Lynn showed me Media Associates' talent blood bank, a room lined with shelving, packed with videotapes, each section delineated by a ranking and a classification by age, sex, and race. She told me how her company went all over the country making tapes of people, rating them from one to five stars, five being tops. The basis for the ratings seemed to be whether or not someone "jumped out at you" with a positive charisma.

Of course, some degree of charisma is necessary to do well in television. But I believed real and lasting charisma comes more from the ability to project a genuine intelligence.

I noticed that the classifications in the talent library included "white male anchors, aged 40-50." There were many tapes on that shelf. There was no comparable category for women. Briefly glancing at another shelf, the one entitled "Oriental Weathermen aged 25-30," I knew I had seen enough.

By then, it was time to go on to our lunch date, which was

affable enough. I never felt any passionate hatred toward Lynn Wilford. I was always polite, although the banal parameters of her thought process were often to stretch the boundaries of my tolerance. During lunch she sought to gain my confidence by telling me that Scott Feldman would be very difficult to work with. She guessed that he would do his damndest to make me look inferior to him. She told me that Scott resented even the slightest suggestion about his "communications" skills. She hoped that my personality and professionalism would help him ease up, become less cold, and a good team player. I told Lynn that Scott had not seemed that difficult to me, and that I hoped we would have a chance to develop real teamwork.

Back at Media Associates, Lynn wanted to show me some tapes. First she played the audition tape that Scott and I had done. Generally complimentary, she told me how all the consultants and the Metromedia people had agreed what a "real winner" they had found in me. Then Lynn showed me a tape of anchorwomen from all over the country, one after another. It was uncanny how they all looked the same, talked the same, and wore variations of the same clothes and makeup. Chicago looked just like Cleveland, looked just like Miami, looked just like Denver. Just as I began to drift off, someone with some spunk popped up. She seemed different, intelligent, streetwise, and spunky. "Let me see her," I said to Lynn. "Oh no," said Lynn. "I don't want you to see her, that's Sue Simmons of WNBC in New York. She's much too assertive!" With that remark and a well-manicured finger Miss Wilford flipped off the tape machine.

I stifled the urge to ask her how someone who was condemned for being "too assertive" had made it to the top of the nation's anchor heap. WNBC is the NBC affiliate in New York City, one of the biggest stations in the country. Sue Simmons was their ratings star.

As the afternoon wore on, Lynn took notes on a clipboard pad about my perceived strengths and weaknesses. Expediting the process I told her I felt my strongest suit was in getting stories. When she asked me about physical appearance, I told her I was neither a beauty queen nor a monster—a five on a scale of one to ten. "What they want from news is news, Lynn. Most Americans aren't models." I relayed to her very carefully how the appearance aspect had been negotiated before my agreeing to come to KMBC.

She implied she understood and agreed with my priorities. She said she looked forward to being helpful in any way she could. Helpful, I thought, helpful if I were deliberately looking for aggravation.

Finally our session ended and I headed for Kansas City and my new apartment. I pulled up in a taxi cab to a sagging structure only partially disguised now by dirty snow. My god, I thought, this can't be the same place I rented. Ramshackle was a kind word to describe the building. My apartment needed a good scouring, which I gave it, suspecting I would not be there long.

I hadn't wanted to spend very much of my salary on living quarters. I didn't plan to be home much, preferring to spend a lot of time on the job, working on stories and series, as well as anchoring. I had hoped originally to save money to complete a very special private project. I wanted to assemble a video documentary on the life and works of a friend, the late poet Kenneth Rexroth. A year before, I had taken my savings and taped several hours of Kenneth in conversation and reading both prose and poetry. We had just finished when he suffered the first of a series of ultimately fatal strokes. Generally considered the father of the Beat Generation of poets and the greatest Western writer adept in Oriental verse, Rexroth had held salons for decades. Writers and poets and musicians made lively contributions to these evenings, usually on Mondays. I was in the last circle of people in his last year. We would take turns reading our works for the group and exchanging questions and critiques. Kenneth had chosen Santa Barbara for the last part of his life. The scenes in my video had been shot at his Montecito cottage tucked in among eucalyptus trees and surrounded by meadows filled with nasturtiums, Japanese chimes tingling in the breeze. I had been fortunate to record those last images and words of a great literary figure and wanted to share those moments with his many students.

But despite the compulsion to save the money to finish the Rexroth project, the Kansas City house was to prove to be just a little too funky. Cinching that impression was a very nice tenant on the the first floor who had a constant stream of male visitors at odd hours. When I was awakened the third time at 2 A.M. by some guy drunkenly pleadingly, "Gloria, Gloria, open up, baby!" I decided I definitely needed a different place to rent. I would look for one, but in the meantime there were even more pressing concerns.

I did a week of field reporting to get acclimated to the assignment and production procedures at the station. I learned that involuntarily hydroplaning my car on snowy streets could be a thrill in itself, a sort of cold woman's substitute for surfing. I was interviewed by a pleasant man, Steve Nicely, the TV critic for the *Kansas City Times,* one of the city's two major dailies. The station had set this up to help promote their new newscast and new co-anchor. KMBC took out large print ads which touted Christine Craft as being "fresh from a California anchor desk." The following Monday, I was to make my debut on the evening news as Scott's co-anchor.

My wardrobe at this time consisted of several silk blouses, some suits, and a few dresses. I usually wore pearls or a simple necklace. My clothes could not be described as elaborate or extravagant, but they weren't cheap either. I dressed at a level comparable to the way I dressed when I had auditioned. There should have been no surprises. I had given them no reason to expect a synthesis of journalism and haute couture.

The first week on the air in any new anchor job is like a shakedown cruise. KMBC, unlike most stations its size, did not use floor directors to give us critical visual cues. This was a Metromedia budget-cutting method of directing a newscast. It is extremely treacherous for the director in the booth to have only ill-fitting ear pieces and a squawk box to communicate with the people on the set. The directors at KMBC were some of the best I'd seen. For the anchors, the tape holding the earpiece cord would frequently become unstuck from the back of one's jacket or even neck hairs. This happened usually mid-sentence at the beginning of a story. The trick was to balance these sensations with attempting to attain credibility.

There we were on the set, Scott and Christine, Kansas City's new anchor team. Just in the wings stood Ridge Shannon and R. Kent Replogle. Because of their presence during most of the very first newscast, I found it difficult to concentrate. Ridge and Kent conferred with each other in loud whispers, then stared at me, then conferred again, this time both staring and gesturing in my direction. It takes a great deal of confidence to be an on-air person. It can be disconcerting, to say the least, when people just out of camera range are obviously appraising you.

Was it just first night jitters? Was I being paranoid? How did I know they were talking about me? Immediately after the newscast, Ridge took me aside by the arm and said, "I don't know how to tell you this, but did you know, well... did you know that one eye is smaller than the other, and that your jaw is square?" The fun was about to begin.

All of a sudden Ridge Shannon had discovered my asymmetry. I silently formed a question never asked. "Why, Ridge, didn't you know that I've had extensive plastic surgery since the first time we met three weeks ago? Isn't it amazing how quickly the scars have healed?" Instead, I reminded him of our several discussions about appearance before I had taken the job. At this point, he seemed to back off, saying quickly that my delivery had been good and that the newscast had seemed both credible and authoritative. I didn't think it would be too wise to ask him what facial symmetry had to do with good journalism, but I did tell him that I was not then, nor had I ever been, nor could I ever be an anchorclone. He shriveled at the word, and asked me not to use the term again in our conversations.

Despite these jarring moments, I was really beginning to like Kansas City. It *was* a nice town with nice people. The plains experience was so different from my more typical California coastal habitat. I was entranced as I rode shotgun with my cameraman through two hours of winter wheat to get to Topeka to cover the openings of the Kansas legislature. The grainy undulations offered a new version of natural wonders.

As I did more stories and met more people, I soon was involved in the process of trying to gain real credibility in the community. There was no absence of topics to tune into. If time spent on appearance was less than my number one priority, the management had been forewarned. I had always felt more of a compulsion to get some last detail of a story than to curl my eyelashes or wax my eyebrows. This is not to say I did not pay some obeissance to the visuals. I didn't think anything would be objectionable about silk blouses and pearls. My hair was growing out from the earlier assault of chemicals and had been shorter than I liked. But Metromedia knew of the fact that I was in the midst of growing it out when they hired me. Like everyone else on camera, I daily applied makeup, powder, cheek color, eyeliner, eye shadow, mascara, and lipstick.

But Metromedia had its own "artiste" with a pancake makeup sponge, none other than Lynn Wilford of Media Associates. Flown in on what she described as an "emergency" visit, Lynn breathlessly told me she had barely an hour to do my makeup. Under one arm she carried a sleek black case outfitted with stage makeup.

Whisking me away from an important story I was researching for my producer, she brought me down to the basement studio with its adjacent makeup room. Next she opened the lid of the case and withdrew a dark brown grease pencil. She sat me down and then used the pencil to draw a railroad track down one side my face, complete with crossties. She had only just begun.

3.

WHEN SOMEONE DRAWS a railroad track down one side of your face, you'd better learn to turn the other cheek. I watched in the mirror as Lynn Wilford drew a shorter, more petite track on the left side. She was determined to neutralize the asymmetry of my bone structure, no matter what it took. Emphasizing the word "contouring" with a mock French accent, she whipped out yet another weapon in the battle against reality. Actually, she held two of them, white grease pencils, one in each hand. Pressed for time, she pulled and tugged at my skin, applying twin reverse panda circles around each eye.

Daubing a sponge caked with rancid makeup in some water, she applied two of the thickest coats of pancake I had ever endured. It was literally difficult to speak without cracking this mask. Never had anyone, even at CBS, piled this pore clogging guck on my face with such overstatement. Then it was time for the cheek colour. Have you ever seen anyone blush in triangles? Evidently such unnatural geometry was necessary for a credible news anchor. The ones Lynn chose for me were equidistant, and in a shade best described as screaming vermillion. The next step was to paint dark brown lines down each side of my turned-up nose to make it seem more aquiline. As she dusted on mounds of powder, I found it difficult to catch my breath without inhaling gusts of beige-tone particulate matter.

Moving right along, she came to her favorite area, the eyes. With a changing palette of mauve, lilac, violet, aubergine, and just plain purple, she began creating a dubious orbital maquillage that began just above the lashline and continued up, up and beyond the eyebrow. It would have looked terrific on rockers Annie Lennox of the Eurythmics or Cyndi Lauper. It did not look terrific on me, aging, all American, "natural" type that I was. Just to make her statement perfectly clear, she blackened and enlarged my eyebrows to Victor Mature proportions. That left the lips, but not for long: two-tone lipliner, drawing the pout on permanently, eliminating any semblance of normal expression I might still have managed to muster. Voilà! I was done, and Lynn was gone, off to Tulsa where she would work more of her special breed of magic on another anchorclone, willing or not.

I climbed the steps from studio to newsroom feeling like a zombie. The first person who saw me coming was my friend, Phil French, the chief cameraman with whom I had driven across Kansas. A crazy cowboy with a flair for candor, Phil wasted no words. "Oh my god, what have they done to you now? You look like a Kabuki doll." "Right you are, Phil, have you seen Ridge Shannon?"

Like a worried kewpie, Ridge peered around the edge of his glass office door into the newsroom. I moved quickly and said, "I've got to talk to you about this hideous makeup job. I can barely move my mouth, much less speak."

Ridge agreed that the makeup looked incredibly heavy, but assured me that Lynn Wilford knew all about TV makeup. After all they were paying her fees because they expected her to deliver.

"Ridge, do I have to do the news with this makeup?"

"Yes, Christine. We are paying these consulting fees and we must get what we pay for." He looked a little apologetic that he hadn't told me sooner.

"Ridge, I just want you to know that I am extremely uncomfortable going on the air like this. This is precisely what we agreed would not happen when I came here." He just shrugged. At that, I left his office and headed back down to the studio.

If my presentation seemed a little stilted that night, no

doubt it was in part due to the fact that even Scott had a hard time looking in my direction. By now, the lipstick had found its way onto my teeth. The eyeshadow had worked down into my left contact lens. My pores were screaming. This I could not endure. The newscast ended none too soon. A red-faced Ridge told me to take off the makeup for the eleven o'clock news. Upstairs in the lobby, the switchboard operator told me they'd been swamped by calls from Kansas Citians asking why I had "all that crap" on. Some of those phone calls had apparently even made it up to the sixth floor executive suites. Intercepted there by the redoubtable R. Kent Replogle, they were translated into an executive order. Lynn's makeup job on me had been positively embarrassing. I was to do my own again, sort of. Media Associates would send some charts I could follow in applying the cosmetics.

That matter partially settled for the time being, I stepped out for my dinner break. The makeup had already congealed, and now nearly froze in the bitter wind as I trudged through the drifts across the parking lot and up the next street to the Continental Hotel. An elevator to the eighth floor took me to the Kansas City Athletic Club. I loved to swim in the club's tiled indoor lap pool. As I showered before entering, I scrubbed my poor face, watching the pancake colored water swirl down the drain. In the pool I took a deep breath and slid under water, pushing off from the side into a familiar realm. After a quarter mile, I knew I wasn't going to let these people get me down. I had come to Kansas City to succeed, and I was going to succeed. Most particularly I was going to succeed at the business of covering the stories in the field. The people of Kansas City were not so stupid or provincial as Metromedia's research would later imply. At least, I felt they deserved more than just the illusion that we knew what we were talking about on the air.

When I returned after the dinner break, I found a fat manila envelope in my mailbox. Attached to it was a handwritten note from Ridge Shannon stating that the contents were important reading. I thought it might be a standards and practices manual for the newsroom. Instead, I found *Dress for Success*, the men's edition.

If the emphasis on appearance seemed overbearing, at least the news part of my job was both interesting and involving. Kansas City had all the elements that pique a journalists's obsessions. It had skid row poor and country club rich. It was a company town with one corporation controlling many things politically and socially. That corporation, Hallmark, also did much in the spheres of redevelopment, art, and image. It provided jobs and glittering showplaces. In return, it expected a certain degree of homage from those in power. Its employees naturally dressed for success.

Kansas City also had its share of mobsters, its drug trade, its gambling. It had pot-holed streets and crumbling bridges. It had traditions of plain-speaking Midwestern honesty and great barbecue. It had a charm that was uniquely its own. Plunging in, I did pieces on such diverse subjects as Jerry Falwell's Kansas crusades and the priceless old masters collection of the Baron Thiessen Bornemeiza.

I went out in the field to interview truckers on the verge of a wildcat strike, and to a home for runaway teenagers which the county had threatened to close in the dead of winter. By the time we had unwrapped the bureaucratic red tape, we found that the funds to keep the place operating were eminently available. Airing the story kept the doors open and some confused kids out of juvenile hall. I was honored with a framed certificate of thanks from the boys themselves.

I embraced Kansas City life for all it was worth. One of the local magazines, the *Town Squire*, published a monthly column I authored. In my spare time, I gave speeches to local civic and service groups. In no way did I shrink from meeting the people. After a sweet realtor named Frances showed me a house I could actually buy for $44,000, with only $5,000 down, I considered it seriously. A similar house in Santa Barbara would have been priced three times higher. I never whined about not being in California. With the exception of one admittedly passionate reference to the Oakland Raiders, I never expressed a preference for anything Californian. Still, some people just couldn't forget. "Gee, Christine," the weatherman would say, "I'll bet you miss those big waves in California, surfer that you are." I responded with, "Well yes, Dave, the winter surf in California is beautiful, but I'm glad to be here in the nation's heartland."

Two weeks after I arrived, I found a copy of the Metromedia contract in my mailbox with instructions to sign and return it to Ridge. Right before a newscast, we had a brief hallway discussion where he suggested that I have Bob Hamilton read it before I sign it. For the next two weeks, every time we saw each other, Ridge would ask me if I had gotten to the contract yet. Actually, since I was busy working on stories and moving to a new apartment, I hadn't found time to read the document verbatim in its entirety.

My friend Bob Hamilton was busy in Los Angeles working on a major miniseries for one of the networks. He had been so gracious with his time I really didn't feel right asking him for more favors. One day on the way to work, I noticed the contract sitting on a stack of papers in a box on the back seat of my trusty Fiat. On impulse I signed it in the appropriate spaces and drove to work, turning it in on my arrival. Ridge and Kent had described it as the "standard" Metromedia contract. I naively believed it contained specific references to three changes Bob and I had negotiated. These changes included the rate of pay ($35,000 the first year, $40,000 the second), the length of contract (two years as opposed to the standard three), and the deletion of a so-called "morals" clause, which was unacceptable. It stated that Metromedia could fire a person for doing something privately that *anyone* in the community found objectionable. As a matter of principle, both Bob and I found that very concept an invasion of both privacy and civil liberties.

Had I taken the time to read the final contract more carefully before I signed it, I would have discovered some disparities from our initial agreement. The contract I signed had the length of time correctly stated, but it did not delete the "morals" clause, and it listed compensation for the second year as $38,500 instead of $40,000.

Also notable at the time was the reappearance of Lynn Wilford. Passing through town again, she spent two hours with me describing what she called the illusion of credibility. It was her theory that news viewers decided whether or not to listen to an anchor, and especially a female anchor, based on what colors, fabrics, and styles she used to create an image of authority.

Lynn Wilford considered herself an expert on the subject; she came armed with several zippered binders, filled with illustrations from the latest fashion magazines. "Look at the believability in the lines of that collar!" she'd wax earnestly as we turned to a mannequin in stand-up silk. I, too, enjoy looking at fashion mags when I have nothing else to do. However, Lynn Wilford had pulled me away from background reading on the President's economic message just to be sure I wouldn't miss her *Vogue* cut-outs. At my weekly take-home pay of $415, I couldn't have afforded the items and accessories she suggested, anyway.

We did go over to Macy's together, just three blocks away. Lynn implied that Macy's and the station might do an advertising trade and get clothes for me that way. Since there had never been any mention when I came to Kansas City that I would have to be totally refitted, it didn't seem fair to have to foot such a bill myself. I was amenable enough to the original Macy's idea. It would be great to have a fresh new crop of well-altered clothes to wear on the air. Lynn picked out blazers and blouses and skirts. I reminded her repeatedly of my foot problem, and how it eliminated skirts, but the thought never seemed to stick in her brain. Some of the clothes she selected were acceptable, though not exactly my heart's desire. Having demonstrated the kind of things she thought would help me be accepted in Kansas City, she left town. I was not given money to buy this suggested new wardrobe. A trade had not yet been established with the station. I bought three or four pieces, but certainly could not afford to buy them all.

I wasn't the only person Lynn Wilford spent time with, I learned later. The female weekend co-anchor, Pam Whiting, had also been subjected to the relentless pleasure of Lynn's company. Pam had been a popular broadcaster and news director at a local radio station. Hoping to capitalize on her knowledge of the community, Ridge Shannon hired her for TV. Like me, Pam was not a model or a beauty queen, but a hard-working journalist with a genuine interest in Kansas City. She had a turned-up nose, sparkly eyes, an impish smile, and a voice that no other woman on the Kansas City airwaves could touch. Both a strong individual and a team player, Pam had gone along with Ridge's admonitions to pay Lynn Wilford's advice full heed. She was thankful that Ridge had sought her out and given her an opportunity. But both of them acknowledged that R. Kent Replogle was Pam's cruelest detractor. He didn't think she was weekend co-anchor material, even though Ridge did.

When Brenda Williams, the woman who had been co-anchoring the weekend newscasts for some time, had to have surgery for a suspected cancer, Pam was given the substitute assignment. In a typical example of Kansas City Metromedia management style, they called Brenda in the hospital, told her concurrently to get well soon, and that she had been replaced. Pam was given the job in a sort of probationary arrangement. If she lost enough weight and achieved "consistency" of hairstyle, and wore the clothes and makeup Lynn dictated, then she might be allowed to stay. As with me, the emphasis at Channel 9 seemed to be on appearance rather than on professional reportorial abilities.

One day I walked in to the newsroom and saw something very familiar indeed. Pam was sporting vermillion cheek triangles. She had been plastered by Lynn Wilford with a particularly unflattering shade of thick white makeup. Then she had to tape some short promotional spots for the news. Essentially it was a pitch for viewers to call their own "direct line to The News" with any news tips. The promos did not mention that the direct line was an answering machine only checked every twenty-four hours. Uncomfortable as a hypster for something that was not what it was made out to be, and additionally uncomfortable in the death's head make-over, Pam was staring into space.

She was the kind of person you would expect to see busy, working on stories or pieces or any of the many things related to her job. But not on this day. Seeking to pull her out of the doldrums, I went to her side. "Hey, Pam, feel like talking?"

The pancake cracking, she managed a quiet "meet me by the mailboxes in two minutes." The mailboxes were mounted in a hallway in the back of the newsroom. Since a partition had been erected between the newsroom and the mailboxes it was a quick place to engage in unobserved conversation.

"Are they always this bad?" I asked her. She confirmed my own early impressions with some added details of her own. It seems that one time when Lynn was working her wizardry with the makeup sponges, she informed Pam that she had a number of beauty faults. One of Pam's eyes (like one of mine) was, God forbid, smaller than the other. She added that appearance on air was much more important for women than it was for men. Pam, as a former radio news director, was well aware of what an employer (or direct agent of an employer) could or could not state to an employee under E.E.O.C. (Equal Employment Opportunity Commission) guidelines. She was both appalled and mortified.

The buzzing squawk of the two-way radio broke our mood as yet another car in the field tried to reach the newsroom for further instruction. The radios were another major problem at KMBC. During the entire nine months of my ill-fated tenure, the two-way radios did not function most of the time. Now, a two-way radio, newsroom to car in field, is an essential tool of any functioning television newsroom. They are not difficult or expensive to maintain. The tiny Santa Barbara newsroom where I worked for a number of years always had operating radios. This is where the real communications comes into communicating. I could not fathom why Metromedia was willing to spend tens of thousands of dollars in consultant fees to create the illusion of credible "communicators," yet was not willing to see that the one most vital piece of newsroom equipment was properly maintained.

Soon I was to learn further just how shallow their response to breaking news could be. The Avon Women's Tennis Championships came to Kansas City, and I did several interviews with the better-known players. It was a strange tournament, with Andrea Yeager beating the heavy favorite, the one and only Martina Navratilova. Martina and her friends and most of the crowd couldn't help noting Andrea's father loudly coaching his daughter from the sidelines during the match. After the press conference when Andrea defended her own petulance, we ran her remarks on the newscast.

In good-natured response, a group of the players and officials asked me to join them for dinner and a game of "boggle." They would see who was the greater wordsmith, tennis players or anchorwoman. Dinner was great as I listened to their tales of the tour. My yearly salary was what one of them made in a fair week. After dinner came the word game "boggle" where their mental dexterity astounded me. They explained that they played this game in the locker room, hour after boring hour, waiting to play on tour. That's why they were so good, and I was no match for them! I took a breather, walking over to the plate glass window of their tenth floor suite at the Crown Center Hotel. Just as I did, a loud explosion ripped the night air and a bright fireball rose from the central train switching yard just to the west of the hotel and directly in the line of sight before me. More flame, fueled by some unknown but incessant source, reached at least two hundred feet while a menacing black plume of smoke headed right for the hotel. I ran to the phone and called the newsroom. No one was there, just the recording. Then I reached my executive producer at home and told him of the catastrophe that was occuring in front of my eyes. I urged him to rush a crew, then I called the fire department. They reported that two tanker cars of toxic and flammable materials had collided in the train yard and that the cloud headed for the Crown Center Showplace was probably hazardous. They were looking at evacuation plans at that very moment. I called back the producer and gave him these latest developments. He replied that it sounded like a good story, but that he had already used up all the overtime allotted for that month and couldn't afford to call in a crew. Stunned, I reiterated to him the spectacular events unfolding outside the window. All he could say was that he would think about calling Ridge and getting some approval for more overtime. Incredulous still, I thanked the tennis players and left to try to find out more about the explosion.

The next day, the explosion was the biggest story in town, perhaps the biggest story of the year. The fire was still raging. A major bridge had been destroyed in the original collision. That would eventually mean a rerouting of traffic for over a week, creating huge snarls and many business delays. That night, the other stations had sent crews to cover events as they happened. KMBC arrived on the scene hours after everyone else, shooting daylight footage. The camera man to whom they eventually did pay some overtime told me that management's response had actually been quick by comparison. He contrasted it to the fatal fire just two years before at the Coates House Hotel, directly behind the station. They could smell the smoke and hear the cries of the injured, he said, but no one dared record the event with company equipment. They were already "off the clock."

With a sick feeling in the pit of my stomach, I took refuge in continuing to do the best stories I could. I took comfort from the other reporters and friends I now had in Kansas

City. One of them, Marty Lanus, was a fine and thorough journalist. Ocasionally we covered the same stories together. Marty was the kind of reporter who would spend six hours in some musty archive looking up one little fact that meant making the story correct. She broke and covered all the mob skimming trials, landing exclusive interviews with individuals under indictments, spending her days off doing valuable research. Marty would tell the model anchorette at her station very carefully how to pronounce the names of principal figures in the investigations. She was a reporter's reporter who happened also to be quite beautiful.

As we sat in a courtroom together covering the case of an adopted leukemic man whose only chance for life was the unsealing of his birth records, Marty was amazed at how my station was covering the trial. She had been in and out of the courtroom all day, putting together a background report on the case to be used in conjunction with her live remote interview at six o'clock. I was given no time to do a background report, just a live shot. More importantly, this was the first time the microwave truck had been usable. I remembered ruefully that Metromedia had promised two trucks and frequent live shots to lure me there. In fact, the remote equipment, much like the radios, was only infrequently usable.

Directly affected by this were the front-line troops, the producers who really ran our newsroom. They couldn't reach their reporters and cameraman in the field and they could never count on the live shots.

My early newscast producer, Sandy Woodward, had another problem as well. It was her responsibility to assign the two anchors their equal share of the writing and production duties when they arrived to work at 2:30. There were several instances where having done this, she would find that I had been pulled away at the last moment to meet with the image consultants. Already under extreme deadline pressure, she would have to find someone else to do my job. Always gracious and understanding about the appearance hassles, she understood that our mutual interest was in presenting an accurate newscast, not a fashion show. In both of our perspectives, the emphasis on the latter at KMBC was hamstringing our efforts to accomplish the former.

In addition, *any* woman who worked in that newsroom knew that the climate was discriminatory on the basis of sex. Scott Feldman in one of his surlier moods would insult Sandy's physicality and gender. "You fat bitch!" he'd spew when he didn't get the lead story, or she'd ask him to do something extra in the spirit of teamwork.

At his worst, Scott Feldman was horrible; the rest of the time I liked him. One day when I'd been ordered to go to Macy's to buy a cream-colored polyester blouse to replace the cream-colored silk blouse I had been wearing, I was not available to do the afternoon live news cut-in. Ten seconds out from air time with Scott spritzing his permacoif, the crew yelled at him to get his twitchet on the set. He barely made it and roared out of the studio, all six-foot-four raging, "Where's that girl? I thought you hired her so I wouldn't have to do stuff like this!" I had just returned from the blouse exchange and caught his bellowing. "That jerk," I thought. "First of all I'm his elder, and if I'm a girl, he's an itty bitty baby boy." I went directly to Ridge, who made apologies and promised to talk to Scott about sexist comments.

I was scheduled to spend that weekend at Jackson Hole, Wyoming. Bob Hamilton had a spacious ski house there and I'd been invited along with some other guests. I had never been to Wyoming, and was glad for the chance to talk to Bob about the developments on my new job. When I told him about the "Where's that girl?" incident, he was infuriated. The next day he called Ridge. Expressing his concern that the KMBC environment was sexist, he asked if Ridge had reprimanded Scott about the remark. Ridge assured Bob that he had and had reminded Scott that I was a co-anchor, a co-equal. Yet when I returned from Colorado, Scott never directly apologized to me. It was not the sort of situation that enhanced good teamwork.

Much more cohesive for the two of us was a shared session we had with Lynn Wilford on one of her return visits. We had to take turns reading Edgar Allen Poe's "The Raven" with varying vocal tones. If Scott would read it "hard and authoritative," I would be asked to read it "warm and comfortable." Scott and I nudged each other under the table when she asked us to both read it "concerned," while leaning crossed-armed over the anchor desk, gold pen crooked in index finger, staring sincerely into the camera. I extrapolated in my own mind an imaginary command, "Now try reading it again, once more *without* feeling." It was hard to keep a straight face, and Scott and I agreed that though these meetings had their black humor, they kept us from getting our work done. The real teamwork between the two of us that began to develop was based on laboring elbow to elbow at adjoining desks week after week. It was based on respect for each other's work: the way I handled the local aspects of the Presidential shooting (interviewing Clarence Kelley, former FBI chief), the way he conducted a revealing interview with the former Missouri governor.

Scott showed a good deal of compassion when they decided to institute a fashion calendar, not for the two of us, but for me alone. "Not again!" he'd commiserate, when the Macy's flack would drag in a big black plastic bag of businesswoman togs and I'd be pulled away to try them on. "We're busy, she's busy, we've got work to do, go away," he'd say with cynical disgust.

By about the sixth month, I had agreed to wear clothes a Macy's buyer selected for me. They would be altered, checked for color on camera, and purchased through an advertising trade with the station. I had not gone to Kansas City to fail and even though this new requirement was not in the spirit of our original negotiations, I was determined to be a good sport. I spent endless hours in Macy's trying on combinations of polyester bowed blouses and blazers. It was the Kansas City schoolteacher look, and if they provided it, I would wear it. Though I refused to wear some of the items offered by my "fashion consultant," Maureen Shauvers, generally the clothes were just boring, clonish, and bland. Tapes were made in the studio of various outfits. I tried on one blouse with four jackets, two jackets with twelve blouses. On the air, I wore the clothes pre-selected by Macy's and Media Associates. The Texas firm looked at all the tapes, and the women in the office there decided which outfits best implied credibility. There I was, a California woman, dressed for the Kansas City television news viewers by the steno pool in Texas. It was quite a cross-cultural experience, a real bite of America. Polyester has always made my skin crawl.

What made my skin crawl even more was a meeting I had with Ridge and R. Kent Replogle the day before my one-week vacation in June. I was going to Santa Barbara to join the Summer Solstice parade. They told me they had just gotten their first "focus group" results back from their researchers and that the people of Kansas City didn't like the fact I was from California. Kent said the impression wasn't my fault. They had promoted me that way and the other anchors often mentioned my geographic roots. "But," said Replogle, "all the anchors have been told to cease all mention of California on the air." An impish thought crept to mind as I imagined an evening headline, "THAT STATE, WAY OUT WEST, YOU KNOW OLD WHATZITZNAME, FELL INTO THE PACIFIC OCEAN TODAY...CALI-WHO?"

They also wanted me to continue to work on appearance, follow a more precise fashion calendar, and apparently lure back those viewers who were supposedly turning off in droves.

"Mr. Replogle, if you think I am so unacceptable here, why don't you let me out of my contract? There is an opportunity back in Santa Barbara." In fact, the acting news director at

KEYT had recently called to find out how I was faring in Kansas City. He mentioned that he happened to have an anchor slot open if I were interested in coming home.

"Oh now, we want you to stay, Christine. Both Ridge and I think you can do it. We really do." Replogle gave his best imitation of sincerity and told me he hoped I'd be a winner and not a quitter. I told him I would sleep on it. The next morning before I left for Santa Barbara, I called and told him I was not a quitter.

Back in the classiest part of a certain sunny state, I revelled in the scented air of flowering trees. I paddled out over turquoise swells in a summer ocean, remembering the piss yellow waters of the Missouri. I celebrated my far western spirit by riding a horse in the festival celebrating the beginning of summer. As a member of the famed riding group, "Los Huevos Rancheros," I rode with my fourteen compadres down State Street in a precision mounted drill team act. Never mind that the horses were artful creations in cardboard. Never mind that I wore Nikes with my mantilla. Our spirit, especially our political spirit, was high. We were spoofing the Rancheros Visitadores, a group of male cattle riders who do a one-week roundup every year. Among the chosen riders: Ronald Reagan, rich Santa Barbara landowners, and male political figures who like to pretend they are cowboys. Every year at least one hundred hookers are brought in from Las Vegas to service the cowpokes at the end of their hard ride away from reality. Our parade unit poked gentle fun at these powerful conquistadores. The parade route crowd thought it was great, as fifty belly dancers filled in the space behind us. Huge puppets scraped the sky, all swaying to the captivating sounds of marimbas and drums and bells and carnival fever. Someone yelled my name and a double purple hibiscus landed in my hair. It would have been very easy, indeed, just not to go back.

But I was not a quitter, and so I returned to Kansas City and my job, bound and determined still to cooperate, to be a good reporter, and to be a success. The faith that I could succeed was not a blind one. Considering all the negative odds, I still realized many positive elements about my position. I was getting good feedback from colleagues and viewers alike about the quality of my reporting and anchoring. They were glad to see a female anchor express a modicum of independent thought. I was interesting to them on levels other than lip color or collar crispness.

Over at Macy's, they were busy preparing a fashion calendar for me to follow that allowed no repetitions in a six-week period. Lynn Wilford believed that "it wasn't fair and it wasn't right, but women in the community judge a female anchor more critically than any man.

"The male anchor could wear the same suit three times in one week, as long as he changed his accessories. But, alas, the poor female, her outfit had better be totally different each evening, or the women in her audience wouldn't hear a thing she said."

The audience was to hear everything I said and not care one iota about what I was wearing on the night of July 17, 1981. We had just finished the six o'clock newscast. One of our crews was out taping a feature story on tea dancing. An old tradition had been revived, a sort of TGIF celebration to big band sounds. It was the newest social rage in Kansas City and everybody had been getting into the swing of things in the lobby of the Hyatt Hotel.

First, the two-way radios emitted a desperate wail as our field crew tried to reach the newsroom, followed by overwhelming static interference. Finally via telephone, word came that the aerial skywalks at the hotel had collapsed, injuring those both on them and below. Our reporter, on the edge of hysteria, managed to blurt out enough details so I could write a script for a live cut-in. Scott was rushed to the scene, I to the studio where I broke the first news of the Hyatt Hotel catastrophe to the people of Kansas City. Within twenty minutes, I was on the air again. "First reports from the scene are that there have been no deaths. We have this unedited video back from the Hyatt. We have not yet seen it ourselves." At that, they rolled the tape and the first image called for a less optimistic commentary; a man's body, caught between two concrete walkways with his entrails spilling to the floor. "Clearly from what we are seeing here, the injuries are far more serious than those first reports indicated."

It become a long night for everyone. One hundred and thirteen people would die as a result of the skywalk collapse. The hotel had been built by Hallmark and managed by Hyatt. Had they cared enough to build the very best? During construction the lobby roof had collapsed. The construction company used by Hallmark's subsidiary, Crown Center Redevelopment, was already in deep financial trouble before it even began construction. An investigation which followed the disaster would show that Kansas City building inspectors were extraordinarily casual about their jobs.

All those questions and more would be asked later. But that night, there were just the relentless accounts of mutilation, suffering and death. A crane would lift a slab revealing several dozen victims. A gallant doctor, the first to arrive, would have to perform triage in a situation more horrible than any he had encountered in Vietnam. There were many heroes, as firemen and police and paramedics risked their own lives to rescue victims trapped in the wreckage. Miracle stories emerged, like that of a child found alive under a bloody heap of rubble. But mostly, it was a night of tragedy as the closely knit community of Kansas City watched the newscasts, trying to learn if friends, neighbors, and relatives had survived.

Throughout the night and into the next morning, I'm not sure how many times I went on the air to update the story. Scott had been sent to the Hyatt or actually a hillock across from the Hyatt to do live reports as well. If ever there was a cohesive story to create real teamwork, the skywalk collapse was it. Each of us labored beyond the call of duty to cover that story as best we could.

The next morning as I arrived at my apartment, I was surprised to see my kitchen curtain flapping in a nonexistent breeze. When I got to the door, I saw why. Thieves had broken in. The curtain was moving because the glass had been broken and the air conditioning turned on. My television set, stereo, rented typewriter, vacuum cleaner and two hundred dollars had been taken. Baskets of mail and papers had been ransacked and dumped everywhere. I didn't even care. It was all so desperately unimportant compared to the tragedy of the night before. The police came and surmised, as I had, that the thieves had observed me on the air saying, "We'll be with you with live updates throughout the night." This was one victim they knew wouldn't be home to put up a fight. I fell asleep, a fitful nightmarish sleep.

The next day, I toured the hotel wreckage with the international press corps. There stood the black Louise Nevelson sculpture I so admired. At its base, bloodied Red Cross bandages still remained. Pink balloons once taut with the emblazoned promise "Tea Dancing at the Hyatt" were now fading fast. Concrete dust and the severed heads of yellow mums littered the staircase where slippered feet had pranced so merrily the afternoon before. Pools of drying blood filled the chamber with a sickening odor of death. No one spoke a word as we looked up at the skywalk supports, steel rods with faulty washers that never should have been installed.

I tried to sample community reaction to the disaster from many perspectives. I talked to an electrician who spoke of what a "rush" job the Hyatt had been. He'd been ordered to put eight rooms on one inefficient and sure-to-be-overloaded circuit. When he pointed out that the job would have to be redone, his bosses, who were Hallmark minions, ordered, "Shut up. This hotel has to be finished on time. No questions, just do as you're told." I talked to a plasterer who watched city building inspectors hobnobbing with developers, giving only the most perfunctory appraisal of aspects of the building they should have spent days examining.

Within forty-eight hours of the collapse, the Bureau of Standards sent envoys from Washington to check out the wreckage as it lay *in situ*. They hoped to determine the whys and wherefores as well as who was to blame. They asked that the site not be disturbed until their arrival. I remember sitting in Ridge's office along with Scott and the principal reporters and producers. Ridge was on the phone repeatedly assuring someone that he did not have to worry. When he got off the phone, he turned to us, muttering under his breath that Crown Center/Hallmark attorneys had vowed not to touch anything. Therefore, he said, there would be no need to spend the overtime to send a pair of eyes to watch the Hyatt lobby overnight, just in case anyone should try to remove the fallen walkways.

Obviously, none of the parties involved wanted any taint of culpability in the city's worst disaster. The construction company, developers, city building inspectors, all sorts of people were subject to increasing scrutiny. I suggested to Ridge that it would only cost twenty dollars to send an intern to watch the Hyatt lobby that night. He demurred, saying it was a good idea, but not really necessary. Apparently the same sort of pact was made at all three television stations. When the wreckage was moved that night to an undisclosed warehouse, only one still photographer captured the image. Every other news source was left scrambling to find the secret building, but it was already far too late.

Mayor Richard Berkley quickly responded when asked why he hadn't halted the removal of the wreckage before federal investigators could inspect the scene. "Stopped them? It was private property, Hallmark's own," he said. A mere mayor had no jurisdiction even though, of course, he had wanted to intervene. The Mayor quickly appointed a Blue Ribbon committee to determine ultimate responsibility for the horror of the last Hyatt tea dance, something it would never really do.

Subsequently in the first week of August, Kansas City voters denied the mayor a ballot issue he had been seeking.

His sales tax initiative would have raised revenue to rebuild viaducts and fill more potholes. Roads and bridges leading in and out of town had been undercut by serious flooding. Downtown streets looked as though they'd been bombed. What would the mayor do now that his plan to save the roads had been defeated? My cameraman and I spotted the mayor entering the ground floor elevator at City Hall. He consented to an interview. I asked the required panoply of questions about the initiative's failure and then I had just one last question for him. "Mr. Mayor, many people think of Kansas City as a company town [i.e. Hallmark]. If you as mayor were to learn that Donald Hall [Hallmark patriarch] or any of his associates knew implicitly or complicitly of shoddy building practices in the construction of that lobby, would you pursue that evidence with the full strength of your office as mayor?"

Richard Berkley blanched, took a few steps backward toward the elevator opening, and said, "I have complete faith in Donald Hall and his associates." His face now filling with color, he completed the turn into the waiting car, the doors closing at his back. It was my impression at the time that the mayor had perhaps expected this type of question from a male newspaper reporter, but certainly not from a female anchorette. Maybe that explained his non-answer.

Six days later Scott and I were asked to pose for a film crew making station news promos for the fall season. When the station's publicist came into the studio to see how the filming was going, she asked why we were doing the promos separately. The director of the out-of-town film crew said that those were his instructions. "That's not right," she said, "There should be one of them together, it must be a mistake. Do one anyway." We stood together and smiled our credible smiles for what would be the last time.

The next day I was removed from my anchor job. I had come in early to listen to a veteran's narrative I was using for a series on Agent Orange. All smiles, Ridge motioned for me to step into his office for a moment. As he closed the door, his expression changed. He told me to sit down, that what he was about to tell me was "nothing personal." Holding up a thick ring-bound report, he thumbed the pages in front of my face. "We've just gotten our research back. Never in the history of Media Associates has reaction to someone been so negative. The people of Kansas City are apparently more provincial than even we had thought. They don't like you because you are too old, too unattractive, and not sufficiently deferential to men. I know it's silly, but you don't hide your intelligence to make the guys look smarter. For example, people don't like that you know the difference between the American and the National League." He emitted a nervous laugh. Did he expect me to be amused by such news? "I'm removing you from the anchor desk effective immediately. Oh, you can stay on and earn the rest of your contracted salary as a reporter, but when the people of Kansas City see your face, they turn the dial."

I was shocked, stunned, amazed, and horrified. If he had just told me that they were removing me from the anchor job because they didn't like me anymore, it would have been a different feeling. I might have been depressed, but I wouldn't have been this angry. Ridge Shannon had just told me that he was taking away my job because I wouldn't pretend to be stupid in order to make my male peers look smarter. If that wasn't a blatant example of sex discrimination, I didn't know what was. For the moment, I only knew that the situation was clearly unacceptable. Still stunned when Ridge asked if I would stay on as a reporter, I told him I couldn't imagine working in a place where I was apparently so disliked. He told me to go home and think about it over the weekend.

I stumbled home, took a shower, and looked at the movie page. "Raiders of the Lost Ark" was premiering at the Seville Plaza Theater that night. It was just a couple of miles from my apartment and the night was balmy. I ran the distance as the sun set, finding a seat, third row center. It turned out to be a great catharsis. You know the scene where Harrison Ford is running from the giant rolling rock, the villains getting crushed in the nick of time? I imagined two heads being crushed. In a moment of full-bore vengeance fantasy, Ridge Shannon and R. Kent Replogle were reduced to pancake faces. I savored the moment. I knew that if I were to try to stick up for my rights, I would need more than a personal vendetta to inspire me. As I ran home after the movie, I knew I would need facts, friends, and good advice to see me through any challenge I might choose to mount.

4.

"Why aren't you on the news?" began the phone calls jarring me out of an already fitful sleep. Barry Garron, newly appointed TV critic for the *Kansas City Star,* was the first to ask. Instead of sticking my tail between my legs and whimpering homeward, I did the unspeakable. I told the truth. Metromedia was wrong if they thought a woman would never admit to having been told she was ugly.

Barry Garron wanted to do more than a phone interview. I told him to come over. When he arrived, he noticed the fashion calendar I had taped to the wall. It was the one I'd been required to follow at KMBC. He asked if he could take it with him. I was glad to see it go, with its maddening orders for everyday. "Tuesday, July 21...Evan Picone blue-bronze plaid blazer, Bronze Irka silk blouse, White Evan Picone skirt, Single gold chain." How the hell was I supposed to wear skirts with my congenital foot problem? Flashing back on that calendar, before I handed it over to Barry Garron, I noticed that 90 percent of the program had me wearing skirts instead of pants. Try wearing a size 10½ flat orthopedically correct shoe with your average dress-for-success skirt.

The next afternoon edition of the *Kansas City Story* was sold out all over town. Not even the City Hall newsstand could keep it in stock. At KMBC friends told me the article was cut out of the newsroom copy before it was delivered interoffice. Several people brought in street editions anyway. One Kansas City mother meticulously cut out the article and sent it to her middle-aged son, who worked in Los Angeles. She thought he'd find it particularly intriguing. He read it with interest and put it in his file drawer for future reference.

He was Howard Rosenberg, television critic for the *Los Angeles Times*.

Barry Garron had printed his own story along with the fashion calendar and a summary statement: "Ms. Craft brought to her job strong news experience and a dedication to first class journalism. She thinks KMBC made a mistake in hiring her. KMBC's greater mistake was in removing her as co-anchor."

I was to get another boost later that day. My colleagues called and asked if I could meet them that night. After the late newscast we converged at a local hangout and all shared beers and anecdotes. Producers, anchors, reporters, and cameramen raised their glasses in repeated toasts to the fact that someone had indeed not deferred. Scott told me he hadn't quite believed his ears the day I was demoted. Finding me not there when he came to work, he asked Ridge Shannon where I was. Shannon, thinking perhaps that candor between two men superceded other ethics, told Scott that news viewers nationwide would only watch news delivered by women if the women were young and pretty. He added that my alleged lack of those qualities in Kansas City made the viewers dislike Scott too. Further, the Media Associates research warned frantically that though they hadn't already, the ratings were sure to plummet soon.

Scott smelled a rat. He remembered, as I did, a conversation that we'd had on opposite sides of the makeup mirror just a few weeks before. Flush with mutual admiration for each other's professional abilities, Scott and I knew we had, as a pair, done the tightest newscasts of any station during the Hyatt tragedy. Our sense of teamwork was becoming real and earned, not contrived and illusory. As he hair-sprayed his part, I brushed an eyebrow and we both began to talk at once. "If the ratings don't go up this book (July), then the conclusion is obvious; quality is insignificant in gaining viewership."

"I agree," I answered. "Conclusively we kicked tail in July.

Mark my words, those ratings will be up. I'm sure of it." I remember having a sixth sense they would.

Apparently no such optimism infected Replogle or Shannon. Though the ratings had been due less than a week after I was removed, they couldn't wait to check their research against the only statistic that actually counted. The afternoon after my KMBC staff goodbye party, Ridge phoned and asked if I could meet Kent and him at the Kansas City Club in fifteen minutes. They had received that morning an urgent mailgram which I had sent them. In it I had stated that I remained ready and willing to perform the duties for which I had been hired, i.e. co-anchor of the weeknight newscasts. It also told them I would pursue legal remedies if forced to. On the phone I told Ridge I'd try to make it downtown, but that it would take longer than fifteen minutes. My car was having major surgery and I'd have to call a cab.

During the half hour ride downtown, the driver told me an interesting tale about the Kansas City Club. Seems the all male establishment had just begun opening its doors to women on something like alternate Wednesdays, but only on the mezzanine. As we pulled up half a block away, I saw my two antagonists standing under the men's club awning. They ushered me in through the revolving door and politely led me to wingback chairs on the mezzanine.

Kent spoke first, "We think you're just trying to get back at us." Ridge nodded in mute assent at his side.

I listened and then let them hear the gist of my anger. "It is your prerogative as a manager to fire me if you don't like my work, but you cannot fire a woman because she doesn't hide her intelligence to make male peers look smarter. That is sex discrimination. We have a civil rights act in this country and sex discrimination is an unacceptable practice. I am willing to return to KMBC and continue my contractual agreement until the first option (December of that year) as co-anchor of the nightly news. If you had removed me because you'd decided you just didn't want me, you should have merely said so. What Ridge Shannon did say was pure and simple discrimination. I will not accept it. I will pursue my rights. You can in no way show that my presence at KMBC has caused any decrease in revenue engendered by the news operation. You did not hire Christine Craft sight unseen. You made every pledge not to alter my appearance when you induced me to come here in the first place. In fact, your practice has been entirely the opposite of those agreements. We can settle this now, if you'll let me come back to work." Ridge grew agitated and burst out with, "I never said those things!" Kent watched his face as I quietly but firmly answered, "Yes, you did."

The conversation continued for another ten minutes. "You can't fight us," said Kent. "We're Metromedia, we have teams of corporate lawyers, and we win every case. You're a soon-to-be-divorced woman going back to a small town. [Lorenzo and I had yet to sign the final papers.] How will you ever raise the money to fight us?"

This was a good question, but I remained unstymied. "I don't want to fight you or Metromedia, Kent. I want to continue doing the job I was hired for. On the other hand, if you deny me my civil rights, I will not just disappear. If I have to raise the money to fight you, I will do so."

Kent was clearly getting frustrated. I could stand my ground as well as he could. "We can afford to keep your back against the wall, forever," he blustered.

I never doubted that he meant it, but I always questioned the relativity of the word "forever." Could it mean that I would be blacklisted "forever?" But after all, if I was already "too old, too unattractive, and not sufficiently deferential to men," I had nothing to lose.

I also had no desire to become a litigant. When Kent softened his approach and inquired, "Would you be amenable to a settlement?" I had a low-key response. "I'd be amenable to having a settlement discussed with my representative."

That pretty much ended our tête-à-tête. They led the way down to the front doors of their club. I walked outside first. They followed, but once we were all out, I remembered something. "Well, see you later, I forgot to make a call." With that I walked back into the building, leaving them outside with very quizzical expressions, the whup-whup of the revolving door wafting a touch of my perfume back in their direction. Inside I marched across one of the forbidden floors straight to a pay phone. When the cab company answered, I specified a woman driver. A little feminine energy was needed right at that point.

Actually, there were all kinds of good energies being focused my way as I lived out what were to be my last days in Kansas City. There were a lot of letters to the editor at the newspapers and viewers flooded the station with telephone calls. Secretaries and switchboard operators saved the phone lists and the mail and made sure I got all of it. Passers-by would stop me in the street and say how they had enjoyed my work, that my appearance was just fine, and that I should pursue my rights against the bastards at Channel 9. In the *Times*, an editorial cartoon by the talented Lee Judge stated things succinctly. The cartoon consisted of three frames. In the first frame was the executive sixth floor office of KMBC Metromedia, Channel 9. Two men were talking, their voices heard from outside the window: "Well, I guess we'll have to find somebody to replace Christine Craft."

Second frame: "They'll have to be young, pretty, and deferring to men."

Third frame: "Well I guess that rules out Walter Cronkite."

Also providing a significant energy boost was a column by the *Kansas City Times* television columnist, Steve Nicely. Just one week and a day after my demotion he wrote: "No grounds for the firing of Christine Craft from her news anchor position at Channel 9 are apparent in the latest Arbitron ratings. Advance results from the July survey reveals an improvement in Channel 9's relative position against its competition at 10 P.M." Nicely also reported that Channel 9 was the only one of the three in Kansas City which did not lose ground in the ratings. For the first time in three years the Nielsen July ratings showed Channel 9 in first place at 6 and 10 P.M. in July, the last full month I had co-anchored the news.

In fact for the first time in three years, Channel 9 had achieved first place ratings. I had in no way hurt their "products" or their profits. Indeed, it could well be argued that I had helped both.

Acting once again as my representative, Bob Hamilton made that point to KMBC. "Hire her back; you're first in the ratings. Christine has done an excellent job. The community recognizes that and will watch Channel 9 even more as a result. Christine wants to return to her anchoring duties and is willing to get back to work with no recriminations."

Kent and Ridge must have known that Bob's advice was shrewd and probably right on target. But it would have been much too hard for them to nip discrimination in the bud and admit to having made a mistake.

Metromedia made its first settlement offer through Bob. They offered to pay me $9,500. That was approximately 75 percent of the amount I would have made through the rest of the remaining year. Seeing that I had been robbed in more ways than one, the offer didn't seeem totally improbable to consider at first. Then they added the one little phrase that would become the perennial camel's straw. "We'll give you $9,500," they said, "plus we'll throw in the clothes." They just never seemed to learn.

I had the clothes all dry-cleaned and delivered via courier on Sunday afternoon to the news director's desk. When he came in to work on Monday, there on top of his copy of the fashion calendar under glass were stacks of bowed polyester blouses, credible puce and plum blazers, and those matching skirts that looked so stunning when coupled with orthopedic footware. Scott told me later that when he came into work and began writing some of the evening stories, his concentration was interrupted subliminally when he noticed my pre-selected anchor togs hanging on the coat tree in Ridge's office. "Oh my God," he thought, "it's the chrome yellow jabot blouse, it's the J.G. Hook madras blazer, the clothes, all of them, she's given them back!" He suppressed a chuckle as he continued writing. If he had any doubts that I meant business, seeing the anchor-clone togs so arrayed on Ridge's peg eliminated them.

KMBC sent me a mailgram stating that if I didn't report to work as a reporter by the following Monday at 9 A.M., I'd be considered in breach of contract, and that Metromedia would consider legal action against me. Reporters usually went to work by 9 A.M., not anchors. Nonetheless, I showed up Monday right on time and walked down the hallway to the newsroom. As I passed the PM magazine office, someone stuck out a hand in the thumbs up gesture. I kept walking, finally through the entranceway to the newsroom itself. Ridge Shannon stood just outside his office, other male reporters and producers were positioned in the room to be witnesses to what would happen next. I stopped about two paces in front of Shannon and said very clearly to him, "I am reporting for work as the co-anchor of the six and ten o'clock weeknight newscasts." Shannon replied that I could not work as co-anchor, but that I was welcome to stay on as a reporter. With that I turned around and left the station. I was never to go back again.

Up to the very end, I did want to return to the job I had been hired for, no matter how difficult that might have been personally. Now that door was finally closed. I consoled myself with the realization that my options would only be as limited as my own imagination. The station in Santa Barbara had offered me my old job back, anchoring two newscasts a day. I was already extraordinarily lucky. I had a beautiful place to come home to.

My most immediate task then was to summon up the fortitude to drive my aging, newly repaired Fiat across the flatlands, over the hills and down into the coastal valleys of Santa Barbara. As I began making preparations, friends and acquaintances showed their concern and offered their help. My mechanic not only rebuilt my engine but polished my pea green auto and included a personalized westward-ho roadmap for my solitary trek. He was a transit veteran of some renown. I also sold him an Adler portable with newstype and a sheepskin full-length coat, both for a song. I decided to keep only what I could carry in my car. I sold my sewing machine to a young mother who had never been able to afford one before, and a lot of my own old anchor clothes, like camel's hair blazers and tasteful silk blouses, to a bouncy, redheaded news intern. Household items with and without chic went to several other people.

One young man and his visiting friend purchased a wicker couch with green corduroy seats, a bookcase, and my handmade elipsis of a wooden low table. The visiting friend was a young lawyer working as a clerk for a federal judge in Springfield, Missouri. Mike listened to my story as we sat poolside at my yard sale. He expressed the hope that if I did file a sex discrimination suit, I would do so in Kansas City. That's where the challenge had been made, and that's where it should be decided. I thought his point was well taken. He was the first knowledgeable person other than Bob to give me the legal perspective on just what sort of process would be involved. I understood from the beginning that it would take a long time, a fierce commitment, and some way to raise money.

Walt Bowdine, a local beloved radio broadcaster, ran a call-in show that stretched usual time limits and ran for several hours. It also served to strengthen my resolve. Ninety-eight percent of the calls were friendly, supportive, and urged me to press for my rights. You can't please everyone, though, and some said they hadn't liked my appearance. "She looks like she's been ridden hard and put away wet," said one. "She looks like forty miles of bad road," offered another. Most thought my appearance was just fine and quite a few found it much better than that. The radio show concluded when a fourteen-year-old girl called in. "I really liked Christine Craft," she said. "She was the only woman anchor who did stories herself, she was bright and professional. In fact I wanted to be just like her. But now that I've seen what's happened to Christine Craft, I think I'll cancel my plans to go to journalism school and sign up for charm school instead. Thank you."

The die was cast. I was morally committed to seeking justice. My closest friends all said goodbye, presenting me with a bottle of wine attached to ten metallic helium balloons. I fit myself into the remaining space in the front seat and looked up at a midnight full moon. Someone tied the balloons to my car's antenna. They reflected the lights of the moon and the city as I cruised on to the Southwest Trafficway headed west. I passed Crown Center, where the moon hung for just a moment over the silhouette of the infamous Hyatt Regency. At the exact split second I passed, aligning my car with both moon and building, a tear drifted onto my squarish chin and the balloons snapped free. With a red and silver bon voyage, I was on my long way home. I was also truly alone.

I cranked up the Rachmaninoff on my car stereo full blast. After the Van Cliburn would come the Chrissie Hynde. I had a full range of emotions pent up from being too nice too long. I would stop four times to buy new tapes as I lurched homeward.

I stopped the first night at a Kansas farm house belonging to one of my "fans," a fifty-two-year-old schoolteacher who kept a satellite dish planted in the middle of a field of sunflowers and marijuana. For the rest of the trip I stopped briefly at roadside motels to sleep long enough so that my eyes could stay open for another twelve-hour stretch behind the wheel. I couldn't seem to sleep longer than four hours. Fueled by large cups of truck stop coffee and driving a little car that wouldn't quit, I got as far as Williams, Arizona, before running into real trouble. As I sputtered to a stop on an uphill grade in the middle of a chilly downpour, two students and an elderly Good Samaritan helped me get into town where a new fuel line was installed.

Further on down the road came the great desert which, according to the radio, was basking in 117-degree heat. I spent many hours at roadside water stations, waiting to fill my bedeviled radiator. Other travelers stopped too, some sharing their ice or a cold soft drink. It was actually quite pleasant to worry about surviving the desert crossing, really far more interesting than the convoluted machinations at KMBC. I forgot for the moment the dubious ignominy of having been labeled too old, too ugly, and too smart.

At dawn when the heat was already too piercing to allow much breathing, I crept into aptly named Needles, California. As I tried to negotiate a side street to get a popsicle, my foot got no response from the gas pedal. In unwavering neutral I slid into a repair shop that thankfully happened to be right there.

Lo and behold, a well-muscled mechanic, with the visual appeal of Sam Shepard and what would prove to be the technical knowledge of Andy Granatelli, stepped out from the shadow of the doorway and offered his assistance. Ordinarily, I might have acknowledged a certain degree of lust in my heart at running into someone so appealing. Very little would have stifled my innate curiosity about such a highly attractive individual. But this was different—I found myself feeling withdrawn and self-conscious, instead of gregarious and confident. It wasn't just the situation of a potentially terminal difficulty with my car, stuck as I was in the middle of nowhere. It was an after-effect of my Kansas City experience. Though I may have dismissed intellectually the statement that I was too unattractive, I nonetheless felt in the core of my psyche that something about my face was difficult, if not monstrous to behold. It's hard to be even mildly flirtatious when one is troubled by such a crippling point of view. The space and time and people that had intervened since that unfortunate day in Ridge Shannon's office had been a buffer of sorts. Now the dimensions of a deep personal wound were beginning to reveal themselves.

Mending the linkage between the accelerator pedal and the Fiat's innards with a prayer and some baling wire, my handsome savior sent me off back onto the highway. I had only a few hundred miles to go before reaching the coast. He charged me nothing and gave me gentle reassurances that at least that part of my car would probably not act up again. I thanked him with an averted smile and a melting popsicle. It was still hot as hell, but I felt a chill of absolute aloneness, as if I wasn't quite sure anymore of who I was.

From Needles to Barstow and beyond and finally into the Los Angeles Basin, the car valiantly limped homeward. Hitting the L.A. freeway system in the Stygian 3 A.M. morning was enough of a jolt to keep me wide-eyed all the way to Santa Barbara. Taking the longer coastal route from Santa Monica northward gave me the dawn's light gift of golden waves lapping on a wonderful and familiar shore.

It was still before 8 A.M. when I pulled into Bob Hamilton's long driveway. The terra cotta of his two story Spanish hacienda was accented by the splendor of verandas dripping with bougainvillea. I was home at last, or at least for a while. Bob had extended an open invitation for me to stay in the guest wing for as long as I needed. I stumbled out of the car, took a visual swig of his private beach, and made a weary beeline for the bedroom. Soon, luxuriating in the profound depths of a perfect down-filled quilt, I fell into a marathon sleeping session. I was awakened only partially when I heard the cook ask, "Will there be two for breakfast?" I didn't hear the answer.

Some significant time later, when I finally did awaken, it was to find Bob's arms around me, to hear his welcoming words. I was all right, I had survived the journey intact, and what's more, he was proud of me. I had wounds to lick, it was true. But this was a lallapalooza of a place to do it in. I looked like death warmed up: deep, black bags, cloudy stain-stressed eyes, a runny nose, and painful neck spasms. I had to recover quickly because I was due back at my old station to resume anchoring in just two days. Spying some gold-wrapped Godiva chocolates, I said to myself, "So what if I get a pimple from eating these? I deserve one, I'm ugly anyway and I have a reputation to live up to."

As I crunched down on a semisweet morsel with filbert, I ambled out into the morning Santa Barbara light, to the edge of my own veranda. I soon noticed something that filled my whole body with delicious anticipation. A parade was being hosted right outside my bedroom window. Around the point of coast known as Miramar, perfect turquoise tubes were marching through in precise episodic sequence, begging to be ridden. None of the locals had yet paddled out. I was into my purple and black wetsuit in a flash, breaking off the one still-polished nail from my old anchorette job. A quick hop, skip, and jump down some rocks and onto the beach—I could soon feel the wonderful pull and stretch in my shoulders and arms as I slowly paddled out through the inside sets and into the lineup. My inner thighs, semi-atrophied from too much driving, protested as I straddled my board to wait for the right wave. When it came, I dropped in late, staying back in the hook as the curl hovered over my outside shoulder. Looking down the face of the wave, I could see the reflection of the colorful beach houses that lined the shore speeding past. I climbed into the center of the wave, locked into the slot as it were, and rejoiced in the beauty and power of that special place where there is no dress code. By the time I kicked out at the end of the wave, I was feeling much better indeed.

Bob supplied me with megavitamins, his bright sense of humor, and infinite friendship. Renewed colleagues at my old Santa Barbara station were marvelous, asking some questions but not too many. They knew I worked hard, that I loved the community and the little station on the hill. I had never segregated myself from the engineering or production staffs at KEYT as a news "star." The hospitality of some of those veteran employees was heartening as I returned to take my co-anchor post side by side with the inimitable King Harris.

Both of our names, Chris Craft and King Harris, sounded totally contrived. Neither was. My parents almost named me Erica, but decided at the last moment to stick with the matrilineal tradition of "Christines." Harris's family was old-line California aristrocracy, the kind of family where a first name like King doesn't seem unusual. The Kinger, as we called him, was a paragon of preppy loyalism well before it enjoyed the current chic. He had been a preppified "sixties" rebel. At one time he was a long-haired drummer playing with a number of bands including Ricky Nelson's. Later he went to Vietnam to serve as an Army intelligence officer. Surviving that, he came back and became a preppy again. He was to the manner born. His zany streak showed up on his socks. His favorite pair had little tiny TV sets intaglio'd all over them. I was in the habit of seeing his socks because he usually took off his prep loafers at night when we prepared the eleven o'clock newscast. His faithful dog Huntley, a golden retriever with half a tail, would lie at his stockinged feet as we worked. KEYT was small enough to allow us the freedom to be ourselves, to do our best work, even to bring our dogs for protection and companionship at night up on the hill. We didn't have editors or producers or interns to help us get the late broadcast on the air. We did it all ourselves with a sense of professional accomplishment night after night.

Always just outside our newsroom was the glistening Pacific lit by numerous oil platforms. From our hilltop we could see all of Santa Barbara, the traffic grids and the flow on Highway 101; we could see accidents, fires, and explosions often before anyone else. This often gave us a news edge and always a sense of wonder. The view was breathtaking, every day and night. It was the best of all possible worlds and we both appreciated it.

It certainly helped being where I was with the people I was with, but I also found I had some major problems going on the air for the first six months after I returned. I'm sure it was that part of my psyche still responding to the insults of KMBC. I could feel a distinct undercutting of my self-confidence. I perhaps over-compensated by being even more serious about the content of my work. Though not a wrong direction to err in, it made me a distinctly more sober newscaster than before.

Another sober experience occurred on the home front as well. A long distance phone call from TV critic Steve Nicely in Kansas City woke me out of a deep, early morning sleep. "Well, I don't know how to say this," he said, "but I was at a cocktail party the other evening and... well, the rumor is that the real reason you were fired was, well, because... because you were not only a lesbian, but an out-of-the-closet one. Is that er... true?"

I rubbed the sleep from my eyes and put one to him. "Tell me, Mr. Nicely, was this a party with Metromedia executives in attendance?" He stuttered a weak reply in the affirmative, warning me he couldn't tell me who they were. "That's all right, Mr. Nicely, you tell them for me, very un-anonymously, that I am not intimidated by their innuendoes. I will pursue my rights." Apparently other gossip in Kansas City had me "openly dating black men," and "openly addicted to drugs." I made sure that Nicely understood that I was not in or out of any closets, that I didn't discriminate against my friends on the basis of race, age, gender, or sexual preference, and that Metromedia could stick its prurient interests up someone else's proclivities. It was a difficult conversation, at best, and I finished it more determined than ever to proceed.

Bob Hamilton connected me with broadcast and entertainment attorneys in Los Angeles for a top-flight briefing on procedure in seeking redress for the wrongs I perceived had been committed against me. A team of them played devil's advocates as I told the facts. When we had finished a lengthy interchange, I had a concrete idea of my legal options. Since the sex discrimination aspect of my experience had been the most galling part of what had happened, it was imperative to understand how to make a federal case and get a federal question answered. Was it acceptable for a woman to be told she had to hide her intelligence to make her male peers look smarter? I knew clearly that it was not, that it was plainly a violation of both the spirit and the language of the Title VII portion of the Civil Rights Act of 1964. By the time I left the L.A. lawyers, I knew that I needed to file a claim with the Equal Employment Opportunity Commission.

I went to their Wilshire Boulevard offices with a preordained understanding that they were bureaucrats who would do their best to convince me I didn't have a case and should forget trying to file one. I had been perfectly forewarned that the EEOC, especially under the current administration, does its best to do absolutely nothing. I also knew that I had the right to file charges with them, a right that they could not deny.

The process at the EEOC was exactly as it had been described to me. After three hours, mostly spent sitting in waiting rooms, I finally was able to dictate my complaint verbatim to an officer who begrudgingly did the minimum his position required. I had no expectations that the federal agency would do anything to see that its own standards were defended. I was not to be disappointed. It was a well-known political fact that under the Reagan Administration, the number of cases pursued by the commission had plunged radically to less than a quarter of what they had been under Carter. One needed private counsel and a right-to-sue letter from the EEOC to proceed in any sort of meaningful way. The right-to-sue letter took one year to receive from the EEOC. Once one had it in hand, within certain prescribed time limits, a lawsuit could be filed in federal district court. I had a choice of venues for filing the suit; it could be done in any city where Metromedia did business. One of these many cities, Los Angeles, would probably end up costing me less. Some sparkling West Coast legal talent was available as well. But it seemed imperative that the case be tried at the source—Kansas City.

Now I needed lawyers, Kansas City lawyers, so I made a trip back to talk to some who had been recommended by friends. In her twenties, fresh out of law school and a federal court clerkship, Sarah Hays was an expert in the intricacies of sex discrimination law. When I visited her, she asked if I would mind meeting another lawyer from her firm, Gage and Tucker, someone with more trial experience. I had no objections. She introduced me to Dennis Egan, just turned thirty with Robert Redford good looks and a Kansas City lineage par excellence. Already deemed by some as a courtroom boy wonder, Dennis combined a terrific personality with immense energy, tenacity, ambition, and a sense of fair play. I told the two of them the procedures I had already followed and they concurred with those preliminary actions. Though I had two other law firms in Kansas City greatly interested in taking the case, I knew the moment I met Dennis and Sarah that they were the duo for me. The three of us understood right from the start that our success in a trial would depend on how closely we worked together over the coming months. They needed to learn about the patterns and practices of TV news, especially those of KMBC Metromedia. I had an immense amount to learn about plaintiff's cases in federal court. Right from that first meeting we began to acquire a team mentality, a mental embrace of mutual righteousness.

Dennis and Sarah wanted the case. Each would have an opportunity to explore his or her own specialties in a suit which raised some fascinating questions on many levels. The law firm of Gage and Tucker agreed to a fifty percent contingency arrangement. In other words, whatever damages were eventually recovered would be shared fifty-fifty by me and the law firm. If we lost, I would not have to pay the legal fees they had incurred acting as a plaintiff's attorneys. In addition, I would be required to pay so-called "out-of-pocket" expenses, no matter what happened. Out-of-pocket expenses included deposition fees, travel expenses, telephone calls, total photocopy and myriad other charges, all of which mount up very quickly.

Realizing that I would have absolutely no way to pay such debts, that my salary in Santa Barbara was appropriate for little beyond subsistence, I had to learn to ask for help. To pay for my lawyer-seeking trip to Kansas City, about one hundred professional women held an impromptu fundraiser at a Kansas City eatery. I was called upon to give a speech to inspire them to reach for their checkbooks. Though it is not easy to ask for money, I knew that I'd better learn how to do it quickly. I fumbled, albeit passionately, through a statement of why I needed their help. The hat was passed and enough money was raised to pay for my airplane ticket home. The symbolism of their collective gesture was perhaps more valuable than the cash itself.

Still more valuable was something I hadn't actively pursued: publicity. It came my way with an intensity I never could have contrived in my wildest thoughts. A very beautiful female anchor in Los Angeles who did the weekend news and reported three days a week for the NBC affiliate in that city was at a party where someone who knew me asked her a rhetorical question. Did she think she'd be able to stay on the air after she hit a certain age? In the discussion that followed, he mentioned that someone he knew was going through a real nightmare because she apparently wasn't pretty enough to do the news anymore. Cynthia Allison knew a good story when she saw one. She got my number and called me. A lot of people thought Cynthia was the least likely person to report my story. She was constantly harassed as the kind of person who had gotten her job solely because of her looks. I had always liked her on the air because she seemed to me to be savvy as well. Not unaware of the power of her own appeal, she had a very realistic view of television news. She was a sort of white-bread Catherine Deneuve, direct from the midwest, with traces of that distinctive flat accent disappearing every day. When we met, she was instantly aware of the implications of the course I was pursuing. It was to be nothing less than a challenge to the broadcast industry's practice of removing women from the airwaves when they no longer fit some mold of compliance, titillation, and cellular elasticity. Even this L.A. "star," this beauty of tinseltown anchorettedom, understood the meaning of my quest. Perhaps she knew far better than most that the smile line just becoming visible in her left cheek would doom her to failure faster than any major gaffe on election night.

Cynthia came up to Santa Barbara with a crew. We did some interviews on the deck of Bob's house with a misty ocean in the background. She taped me doing the 6:30 newscast from KEYT. The station consented when she asked to shoot inside the studio. She asked Metromedia for a response; they had none. The piece she finally aired was well-written and well-produced and just happened to be seen by one Howard Rosenberg, TV critic for the *L.A. Times*. This was the same Howard Rosenberg who had received a little clipping from his mother about the Kansas City anchorlady who had gotten such a bum rap. The next day he drew the clip out of his file drawer. Christine Craft was not an unfamiliar name or face to him. Since he lived between Malibu and Thousand Oaks, he could pick up the Santa Barbara station most of the time and had often watched our local news.

Rosenberg came to Santa Barbara and ended up doing a piece for the Calendar section of the *L.A. Times*. Complete with three pictures, a prominent headline, a reprint of several weeks of the "fashion calendar," the column drew attention. It was an interesting enough story, one quickly made available through the *Times-Washington Post* syndicate to be picked up by major newspapers all over the country. I began to receive quantities of mail and I started to do lots of radio interviews and television discussion programs with formats evolving out of the question, "Why aren't there any female Walter Cronkites?"

It took a year to get that right-to-sue letter from the EEOC and it would be almost another year before we went to trial. In that two-year period, I continued anchoring and reporting the news in Santa Barbara. Local groups asked me to address them; thus I was able to engender many community networks for later fundraising. Under the aegis of the Santa Barbara Women's Community Building Project, groups like the Democratic and Republican women of Santa Barbara County, Business and Professional Women, South Coast Business Network and others helped me raise seed money of nearly $3,000 get closer to trial. It was terrific to see women of different political affiliations and strata of local society get together for a cause that they all could support.

There were other aspects of personal good fortune which helped me maintain my resolve during the two-year period. After six months of staying at Bob Hamilton's manse, I located an inexpensive rental over a garage on a beautiful stretch of beach. My second bit of good fortune came when I rescued a marvelous dog one hour before his death sentence at the county pound. A long haired breed of Siluke, Afghan, Doberman, and setter, Schnaubel, as I called him, was a companion on many a tension-relieving beach run. A terrific watch dog, Schnaubel guarded me and our house with top-flight earnestness. When the station got wind of an anonymous threat to kidnap me, they hired armed guards to watch me for a couple of days. I carried a walkie-talkie for two months so that I would always be in constant contact with the station. My greatest guardian, however, was Schnaubel, always alert, strong, and with that streak of Doberman assertiveness. I purchased a companion for him, a yellow Labrador puppy, one of a litter of twelve born on my beach. Looking at my co-anchor King's dog, Huntley, I impulsively named my new pup Brinkley. This pairing helped keep my attitude light-hearted, at least part of the time.

I also had the good fortune to get a terrific new news director. Carol Breashears had spent many years in both radio and television news. Mid-forties with a no-nonsense attractiveness, she insisted that all of us at the station would benefit by having someone do our makeup every evening before the newscasts. The woman she hired was a Chanel cosmetics expert with fine products and a darling personality. Clara was from Ecuador, and often sang lilting melodies as she applied cosmetics with a touch designed to make anyone feel better about themselves. I could always tell her if I didn't like something she had done. We would work together so that I felt comfortable and natural with my "on-air" appearance. I have never been opposed to working consistently with someone who knows what they are doing to maximize the pluses of my own appearance. Seeing Clara every day was a positive experience, something I looked forward to.

On the news side of things, Carol Breashears and I did not always agree on how to cover a story, but I could always go to her with a point of view, present the case, and get an involved reaction. It was great to work for someone you could learn from, someone who took pride in her job and in making our local newscasts more accurate.

Under her wing, I did a series on toxic shock syndrome, an investigation into the mysterious death of a local woman, special programs on the imminent licensing of a nuclear power plant which sat on top of an earthquake fault, and many other important stories. Compassionate yet realistic when details of my lawsuit began to generate outside media attention, she provided a challenging workplace, which was my first priority. She knew how much I loved my work and made sure that I had plenty of it to do right up until the trial began. Also, she gave me opportunities to take a few days off when the pressure was inordinately heavy or when, for example, I was asked to take part in a televised discussion of my lawsuit on the Donahue portion of ABC's "The Last Word." I was very concerned when just two weeks before the trial, Carol Breashears resigned to take a bigger job in Los Angeles. Her replacement was a woman who claimed to have been a television reporter, when in fact she had not. While she did have extensive experience in radio, she didn't know the simplest technical facts about videotape. She also engaged in subtle personal digs against the departing news director, supposedly her friend. The disparaging comments made me uneasy about what I would have to face when I returned, but, for the moment, most of my thoughts were on Kansas City where it was nearly time for the main event to take place. KEYT graciously gave me a month's leave of absence. This left a week to respond to some of the requests for interviews and to go over some of the pertinent bits of data that Dennis and Sarah had become privy to in the course of depositions and the discovery process in the lawsuit.

They had learned, for example, that the consultant group researched had asked a "focus group" of male Kansas Citians the following question, "Let's be honest about this, she's a mutt, isn't she?" This inquiry was just one example of the type of market research that had led to my dismissal. There were scores of other gems that would later be revealed in the trial. I knew that I would have to deal with intense public scrutiny. Was I mutt or wasn't I? The story would get uglier, as more facts became part of the public record. Could I handle that sort of twisted attention? I knew I had a choice. After all, I had a job. I could simply retract the lawsuit, pay the out-of-pocket expenses, and forget the whole thing. But mutt or no mutt, the issues I knew this trial would raise were well overdue for appraisal, by both the court and the people. I did one last interview before Metromedia asked the judge for a gag order.

ABC's Rebecca Chase was putting together a story she planned to air the first day of the trial. She followed me the week before, as I went to Cleveland to do an interview with America's oldest anchorwoman, Dorothy Fuldheim, age ninety. Dorothy appraised me coldly as I entered her private offices before the taping. Her attitude was one of "Show me you're not just a crackpot, give me one good reason why I should be interested in your plight." I gave her my account of what had happened in Kansas City. She interrupted several times to pose the most difficult questions anyone had up to that point. The person who many would have presumed to be my staunchest ally was in fact the hardest to convince that I was telling the truth. She never gushed approval or support, but quietly in the tone of the questions she asked me, I sensed she knew I was fighting a battle she had won many times over. Her parting shot was lighthearted and encouraging, "I've just signed a new three-year contract. I've just turned ninety. I call that optimism!" With a quick wink, she returned to to her life's work of being simply smarter than anyone who would challenge her right to stay on the air.

If Dorothy Fuldheim was inspirational, then the media crowd that met Dennis and Sarah and me on the first day of trial was awe-inspiring. I knew there would be media interest in a trial that questioned media practices, but there was no way I could have imagined the horde that would turn out on the steps of the federal building in Kansas City. Joseph Stevens, the presiding judge, had ruled in pre-trial hearings that he believed in a jury's ability to ignore publicity and heed his warnings about not reading papers, listening to radios, or watching television during the trial. He thus chose not to sequester the six-person jury which had been selected. Yet he knew from the first day that there would be considerable media attention. How about ABC, CBS, NBC, *Time, Newsweek* UPI, AP, all the local Kansas City stations and papers, and many others including international news services?

As we walked up the courthouse steps in the 100 degree weather, cameras recorded every step as they did each time we exited or entered the building during the entire eleven days of the trial. We, of course, could not talk to them as they shouted questions. Our answers and our own questions would be fielded in the courtroom. The moments of truth had arrived. I felt wonderful, rumors of canine ancestry notwithstanding. I knew that many newspeople just wanted to play up the "sexy" aspect of the story. Was I really too old and too unattractive to do the news? I also knew that others like Fred Graham, the revered legal correspondent at CBS, would hone in on the Title VII issue of the case, the meat of the matter. I knew the local stations including KMBC would be competing to cover the story and that I would be able to watch it all. It had taken two difficult years to get these corporate defendants to court. All their money hadn't kept them out of round one. With all the world watching, we realized that this was going to be one hell of a collective day in court.

5.

IT WAS ONE HUNDRED and four degrees coupled with a merciless humidity which added to everyone's discomfort. Eleven days of trial lay ahead, trial by jury and trial by weather. Carefully I had assembled a wardrobe to suit the occasion, selecting skirts and tops that could be handwashed. A jumbo bottle of Woolite, my travel iron, and a bottle of extra strength roll-on completed the travel pack. Each morning I rose at dawn to press my day's outfit to the accompaniment of NBC News at Sunrise, which carried daily items about the trial. Seen through the steam iron mists, anchorwoman Connie Chung was a source of ironing inspiration, poreless and unwrinkled in an air-conditioned studio.

I was, for the duration, staying at the unairconditioned home of my friend and fellow reporter, Marty Lanus. I had the luxury of a compatible environment, and managed to save money too. Marty had told her station that our friendship would preclude any reportorial involvement on her part. In addition, the judge had wisely ruled that none of the principals could discuss the case until the verdict was in. Marty's sardonic sense of humor was a welcome counterpoint to the seriousness and posturings in the courtroom. We could reminisce about the bad old days when we both had covered the same stories.

Stumbling out of her own bedroom to get ready for work every morning just as I'd be leaving for court, Marty would lean over the balustrade and tell me I looked good. I'd grin appreciatively at her, stunning in her hot rollers, and say thanks. She knew more than most how great the pressure would be, and how everyone would be appraising my appearance. Marty was determined to start my day off right, even lending me a beautiful necklace of pink porcelain calla lilies to wear.

Back in Santa Barbara, my dad was tending the homefront, watching over my garage-top apartment at the beach. The homefront had been sadly weakened by the accidental death of one of my dogs, leaving me with a heightened sense of having nothing left to lose.

Friends, viewers, colleagues and my co-anchor in Santa Barbara sent me telegrams with their best wishes. A news team in Florida sent a T-shirt with a note from Dorothy to Auntie Em. "AUNTIE EM, HATE YOU, HATE KANSAS, TAKING THE DOG. LOVE, DOROTHY." One of my two unions, the American Foundation of Radio and Television Artists, sent me financial support in the form of a several hundred dollar check which literally bolstered me up through the trial's completion.

Forty prospective jurors were questioned by the judge and appraised by counsel. Six were chosen, four women and two men. All were working-class people, none appearing to follow the "Dress for Success" bible. While we waited for the selection procedure to wind down, Dennis and Sarah told me a little about the judge we had drawn. A Reagan appointee and staunch conservative, Joseph E. Stevens, Jr., was in late middle age, very short, and bordering on the roly-poly. He had gained mastery of judicial style by staring down over the tops of his glasses. Generally this technique lent authority to the stern presence emanating from the bench. Judge Stevens didn't seem evil, but he did appear to be set in his ways and very much perturbed at having to try this case at all. Once in a while he would emit a spasm of condescending humor that made me chuckle. But, as Dennis and Sarah relayed the details of the on-the-record conversations held in chambers or at the bench, this man seemed inclined from the start not to allow the jury to hear all of our evidence. In a sex discrimination case where the burden of proof is rightfully on the plaintiff, every bit of tangible evidence would be vital. I was further disturbed to read an item in a local teachers' union periodical. It mentioned that before his federal appointment Joseph Stevens was overheard at a large social gathering saying he didn't think women belonged in the workplace. The author noted my bad luck in drawing Stevens as the judge in this case. Maybe Stevens had just been joking, I reasoned. Surely he must believe in upholding the tenets of the Civil Rights Act.

Earlier during pre-trial hearings I had noticed that the judge certainly seemed compatible with the defense counsel, moving the trial date forward in time to accommodate the latter's plans for an Aruba vacation. Donald W. Giffin was the chief attorney for Metromedia. He worked for one of the major Kansas City law firms, Spencer, Fane, Britt, and Browne. Metromedia had wisely kept its own flock of highly paid corporate attorneys in the background. Some of the major advisors appeared in the courtroom gallery, but there was no telling to what degree they assisted the local firm in preparing its case. One could easily assume, however, that the local law firm would not have to worry about the payment of bills. Their client's net worth, after all, was a respectable 1.45 billion dollars.

Attorney Giffin was short and wore rumpled suits. His stiff wiry hair formed a sandy halo around a face that I understandably found less than cherubic. In many ways he reminded me of the mythical Greek griffin, his upper body not at all matched by the small stature of his local extremities. I noticed that Giffin the griffin had a difficult time pronouncing the middle syllable in "employee." He couldn't say "oy" for the life of him. He had a voice which easily turned raspy and accusatory. But although I found him unattractive, he was no comedian in the courtroom; he had a style which could grab a jury's attention.

Sitting also at the defense table were two other attorneys, Sandra Schermerhorn and Mark Johnson. Johnson was the Missouri version of the quintessential Brooks Brothers preppy:

young, inexperienced and somewhat chinless. The other colleague would be charitably described as the spitting image of Alice B. Toklas. At one point after some particularly sexist testimony that Schermerhorn had elicited, a woman friend of hers stopped me as I was leaving the courtroom to tell me that "Sandra was just doing her job." Really, I mused, I had just been trying to do mine.

Filling out the cast of characters, the judge had allowed Ridge Shannon to sit at the defense table as a representative of Metromedia. Also present was the court recorder, Elizabeth Shinn. Throughout the trial, she exhibited extreme grace under pressure. Assisting Judge Stevens with points of law was his erudite young clerk, Kent Sellers, whose presence was a constant source of reassurance for me.

Also reassuring were the two people filling out our legal team, Carole Vetter and Pat O'Reagan. Pat was our investigator and Carole our paralegal and general factotum. Frequently and above and beyond the call of duty, both of them gave all of their efforts to assure that Dennis and Sarah were not lacking in anything they might need to present the case. O'Reagan possessed both a scowl and a smile you couldn't miss from fifty yards. He took everybody's word with a grain of salt, which was just what we wanted him to do. Carole added some undeniably female pulchritude to our team. I'll never know how she managed to run all over town in her three inch spike heels, but I was extremely grateful that so many times she did. A reporter friend noted with a chortle the irony that our side was so much cuter than theirs.

Feeling somewhat demure in a white Peter Pan collared blouse, a linen blue blazer and cotton skirt, I took the stand as the first witness. No consultant had dictated my attire. Later columnists were to write long pieces on the clothing I wore for the trial. Had I been too casual? Too pretty? Better looking at the trial than I had been when co-anchoring? Those subordinate themes would dominate some minds, while on the stand

Dennis' questions and my answers provided a narrative of the core issues for which I was fighting.

Predictably Mr. Giffin balked when Bob Hamilton was referred to as a "friend," instead of merely as an "agent." He had been both, of course; I had paid him no commission. He had acted as my intermediator because he was my good friend as well as someone adept in broadcast law. Throughout the trial, Giffin would portray Bob as some sort of litigation-loving Svengali, without whose instigation there would not have been this lawsuit.

So, too, Giffin would try to undermine my version of the "standard Metromedia contract." I mentioned that in our discussions we had agreed to $40,000 for my second year, but, as Dennis noted, the contract listed weekly payments that only added up to $38,500. Metromedia had also promised they would remove the so-called "morals" clause which gave them the right to fire anyone who did anything that anyone in the community found objectionable. Metromedia had failed to live up to their agreement, by not deleting the offending paragraph. Actually neither side had a particularly pristine record vis-à-vis the contract. I signed it hurriedly, stupidly, not scrutinizing it verbatim. My stupidity was as notable as their failure to live up to the conditions we had agreed upon.

The defendant's counsel chaffed when testimony demonstrated that Scott and I had been reprimanded differently committing the ultimate anchor anathema: semi-unbridled commentary. In my instance, I'd been greatly perturbed at a report from the White House that a first priority of Mr. George Bush would be to eliminate the Title IX provisions of the Civil Rights Act, which provide funding for women's athletics. I'd blurted out, "I wonder if Mr. Bush has any athletic daughters?" In the aftermath of that rhetorical question, I was summoned into the gloomy smoke-filled presence of the executive producer. Properly chastised, I quickly admitted the error of my ways. Scott had, also on several occasions, made derogatory on-air personal comments about the sudden celebrity of Rita Jenrette, wife of the troubled Illinois congressman. For some strange reason, Scott found it galling that such a woman would "rat" on her husband and then benefit from it. All of us noted Scott's repeated on-air vehemence in remarks about Rita. We could not understand his fixation nor, more importantly, why the station management never told him to cool it. Scott was entitled to his lapses as much as I was, but station management seemed to practice disparate disciplines when it came to evaluating whether a male or female anchor committed the same unacceptable error. In a less than subtle way, it smacked of sexism. This was just one of many examples that would be uncovered during the trial.

Another instance of Metromedia's toleration of sexist behavior (as long as it was male dominance over female) was aired early in the trial. A recounting of the incident where Scott had angrily bellowed out "Where's that girl?" drew a distinct judicial response. As the attorneys haggled at the bench over the admissability of this piece of evidence, I could clearly hear Stevens's comments. He did not at all find the expression "that girl" derogatory; he commented that I clearly was Feldman's junior because Feldman had been at the station longer. When I testified that I would never have called Scott "that boy" even though he was my chronological junior, the judge warned Dennis, "She is doing it again. She is giving these judgmental answers and making her speeches and I am not going to let her do it." From that point on, I had no doubts that Stevens was clearly not on the cutting edge of social reform. I wasn't naive. Not all federal judges were dedicated to eliminating vestiges of discrimination in a country where the laws were supposed to give life to the concept of justice for all. Stevens's behavior showed him to be a paradigm of the status quo. I continued to sense that we would have a difficult time presenting all our evidence.

I had ample choice to observe my surroundings: a few

yards from the bench sat the jury, mute and unreadable. Looking at them, I reflected that I had worked awfully hard just to get to this moment where a jury of my peers could hear everything and decide who was lying and who was telling the truth. These people would hear not just bits and pieces, as in the press accounts which caught only those parts that titillated; they would hear testimony even I would choose not to be present for. I could only hope that this jury of my peers would scrupulously listen to the evidence and form their verdicts carefully. If anything, the attendant publicity probably made them more intent on adhering to their oaths. The buck, after all, would stop at their door too.

On the left side of the courtroom, usually towards the front of the gallery every day, sat a man no juror recognized. He was the only journalist who heard all the testimony in the trial. His employer, the *Los Angeles Times*, was the only news organization that understood that to cover a trial, one actually had to be there. Howard Rosenberg, the man who had written the original article for the *Times-Post* syndicate, was in town for the duration, camped out at his mother's Kansas City house. He wore brand new shirts and looked well-fed. His mom must have been glad he was home, even if it meant he'd spend most of his time in the courtroom.

Channel 9 had hired someone they promoted as a "sex discrimination trial lawyer" to comment every night at ten on the issues and progress of each day in court. I noticed this person's presence for about twenty-two minutes the first day, as long as forty minutes on subsequent days, and a whole hour-and-a-half the day of the verdict. She was a telegenic young blonde, whose trial practice was in personal injury cases rather than in Title VII. Once again I saw how TV news could accord the illusion of instant expertise even to those minimally qualified, just as long as they looked the part. I was to learn later about how this "expert" gathered information about a trial she rarely managed to attend. Nonetheless, she always delivered her commentary from KMBC every night on the late news. Channel 9, after all, had its image to uphold. They were making an extra effort to be perceived as credible.

When Kent Replogle appeared during recesses before his own testimony or when he was allowed to be in the courtroom after the testimony, he often sat next to a striking woman whose style of attire could best be described as "studied." She came in and out of the court room frequently, and I wondered if she lived close by. Her outfits were all expensive and accessorized to the hilt, her makeup heavy and her hair prepared in an intricate style. Often I saw her in the hallways huddled with Replogle and associates. I wondered who the mystery woman could be.

The rest of the gallery included some regulars, trial groupies who for whatever reason find the proceedings interesting. There was also a changing pool of reporters and a number of courtroom artists, each with a distinct style. Some made everyone look horrible, the others looked for the best features, while still others did drawings that looked like no one. These were the images taken from a chamber where cameras weren't allowed, the images that were sent to those on the outside. In one particularly obnoxious set, Dennis, our golden boy, looked like a haggard frothing wretch, complete with a gigantic Adam's apple. We at least found the work of the artist pretty amusing and realized how differently each interpreted the same scene.

In the courtroom the scene itself changed as the days went on. There were faces of witnesses for the artists to draw, as well as giant charts and projections. Videotapes of newscasts and clothing selection sessions were shown to the jury. Not once did Metromedia produce a tape where I "stumbled" over my words, or was less than professional, or made any preferential remark about California. They had professed that I had done these things, but nowhere from their vast archives of newscasts taped during my tenure had they produced evidence to support their claims.

Through documents produced in the discovery process, we

were able to show that from the beginning of my employ, Metromedia and Media Associates had decided that my clothes were "too masculine" and that I needed to purchase blouses with bows and ruffles to "soften the look" of my face. Next, another intriguing bit of Metromedia's newsroom standards was introduced as evidence. It was called a "Standards of Performance" on which I was to be evaluated on five criteria. Of primary importance was the first standard. It read: (1) With lighting established, maintain makeup application as acceptable to Kent or me:

Excellent	No criticism in a month
Good	One criticism a month
Satisfactory	Two criticisms a month

The second standard of performance also concerned appearance: (2) Upon establishing of the dress calendar, will not deviate at all from it:

Excellent	No deviation in a month
Good	One deviation in a month
Satisfactory	Two deviations in a month

Further on down the list of news standards were requests for story outlines and the request that four times a week I critique a competing newscast with a written report to Ridge. I testified that I had never "deviated" from the fashion calendar, that I was a good sport, but that all this attention to appearance and time spent critiquing others was antithetical to the way they had represented the job when they had persuaded me to come to Kansas City in the first place.

When the issue of the station's news rating during my tenure was raised, Giffin attempted to keep the jury from hearing that the news ratings had actually risen during my time rather than fallen, as they would seek to imply. The judge, perceiving that I was listening intently to see if that important evidence would be allowed, warned Dennis, "Will you please instruct your client to stop reacting to questions from counsel and rulings by the Court? I am not going to tolerate it. There will be a mistrial if she sits over there and whimpers and giggles any more."

Whimpering and giggling? I may have been a bit wide-eyed, but nothing more. Perhaps our judge had an imaginative sense of hearing.

During his cross examination of me, defense counsel Giffin showed us all how big his own imagination was. He and his assistants lumbered into the courtroom with a blown-up copy of the contract on its own easel. It was bigger than the actual document by a factor of at least ten.

Perhaps by using it he was trying to imply that this sacred writ was somehow larger than life, more binding than ethics. It was quite a prop for his theatrics, which included patronizing and repeated questions: "Are you capable of understanding this language? Are you capable of understanding that phrase?" Ad nauseum. He was trying to rile me, to get me defensive by an assault on my intelligence, but his technique failed. I didn't get angry, I just answered the question in the affirmative over and over again. I knew that no contract frees an employer from laws governing fraud and discrimination.

When he pulled out old phone records that showed Bob Hamilton and Christine Craft were phone pals, he tried to imply that there was something very odd in the fact that two best friends, one very well off, would call each other frequently. I admitted that I had used the station phone to call Bob a few times and offered to reimburse Metromedia if they would present a bill. What I didn't mention was that other reporters and anchors continually and openly used the station lines to make innumerable calls to other cities and stations in their never-ending searches for other jobs. I had never done that.

The second day of my spell on the stand came to an end. We all noticed as we left the courtroom that the media flock, instead of diminishing, had grown ever larger. Local law prohibited them from climbing the steps of the federal building, yet they clustered in tight quarters at the base of the stairs. Every time we exited or entered, there they shouted questions they knew we could not answer. They followed us to our cars, to our luncheon hangouts, wherever. Every time it happened, I felt the strangeness of being on the other side of a familiar process. Dennis and Sarah, Carole, Pat, and Dennis's wife, Judy, or one of the other partners would take turns being my escort. We kidded each other about the different combinations of the Craft legal team that showed up on the tube or in the paper.

As the days went on and I read press accounts of the trial, I noticed that the deadline structure of wire service news often placed reporters in the courtroom for only part of the day. They would hear, for example, direct examination, but not cross-examination. So very often stories they would file purportedly representing each day in court would reflect only portions of those days and parts of the total story. It was easy to extrapolate that on many stories far more important than this one, the public was frequently denied the whole picture. Besides this inherent weakness in the system, the wire services were as diligent as humanly possible.

They all reported, for example, the salient parts of Bob Hamilton's testimony, including one impassioned remark that didn't put us in a particularly good light. Bob calmly reiterated what he had told Ridge from the onset about my adamant refusal to undergo changes in my appearance. He testified that he had told them repeatedly I was not a beauty queen but a thirty-six-year-old California surfer who had seen too much sun. He affirmed that they had said they "loved Christine's look." Bob also told of his own rather intemperate reply to Shannon after I'd been demoted, the good ratings had come out, and Metromedia had refused to let me finish my job as co-anchor: he had suggested that the issue could become a feminist *cause célèbre*.

On the stand, Bob was contrite, admitting the foolishness of the statement, but also testifying how his dander had gotten up when Shannon had told him in the same conversation that "Nobody ever beats Metromedia." The real irony of it was that Bob was right in the first place. Many journalists, and women in particular, understood that the case raised sticky issues about sex discrimination endemic to the American workplace.

Raising his own sticky issues was none other than R. Kent Replogle. When Dennis asked Replogle to reveal the value of the Metromedia stock he owned, Giffin objected and the judge sustained. Moments later the judge reversed himself and allowed Dennis to pursue that line of inquiry. Replogle responded in vague fashion: "approximately $50,000." He was much less vague about the distinction between his job title as station manager and his actual practice. He apparently "delegated a lot of responsibility" to Ridge Shannon. His testimony as to whether or not he was familiar with the concept of equal pay for equal work was revealing. Both in his deposition and on the stand, Replogle stated that he believed the concept of equal pay for equal work was "a ludicrous concept in the area of talents," and that he believed since anchor people were "unique talents," it was "not just the same person doing the same job" and therefore not an equal pay situation. Throughout the trial the defense would try to imply that somehow the hiring and firing practices of TV newsrooms were above the law. It was Dennis's task to reveal the many chinks in that pompous position.

First there was the issue of the monthly reports Replogle had sent to his corporate superiors at Metromedia headquarters, reports that directly affected the amount of compensation he received as general manager. Despite special jumbo-sized defense-prepared exhibits and testimony attempting to prove that I was perceived as someone who was pulling the station's revenues downward, Replogle had written a cheerily optimistic report: "The first period of the new year" (1981 when I began, through the first three months of my tenure) "was a vastly successful one for KMBC-TV." Later the year he would write: "Year to date, the station continues extremely strong, exceeding profit targets by more than 25 percent and up nearly 32 percent from last year." This contrasted greatly with Replogle's explanation of the charts which, because of my presence, purportedly showed a downward trend in ratings and revenues. Dennis further deflated those claims by pointing out that the glossy graphic props failed to show the important factor of demographics. Demographics, or the statistical characteristics of human populations, are used by advertisers to identify markets and to determine the television advertising time they will buy. Very clearly, Metromedia had prepared those charts, omitting positive information, in a desperate attempt to create the impression that I had hurt them. Perhaps even more interesting was Replogle's admission that the last book taken when I was co-anchoring showed Metromedia as number one in news. Under oath he had to admit that this was the first time in three years they had achieved such a lofty and profitable status. To lessen the impact of that demonstrable fact, Replogle dismissed it as an "aberration."

One of Replogle's theories was that viewer attitudes take some six months before they develop into viewer action. He swore up and down that the "research" showed people had negative attitudes toward me, attitudes that soon would be translated into bad ratings. Using that theory, the supposedly poor showing (*i.e.,* no meteoric rise in ratings) of the first few months of my employ could be attributed not to me but to attitudes as long as six months prior to my arrival. Replogle shifted nervously. He knew that I had caused no loss of revenue, no drop in ratings. All the contrived charts and supposed expertise were being revealed for the worthless paper they actually were.

At one point, Dennis inquired of Replogle if he did any on-air presentation. Yes, he responded, he did editorials, public service announcements, and the like. Without skipping a beat, Dennis asked if it were true that at one time Replogle had told a female newscaster to cut her hair because he thought it was too frizzy. Giffin stormed benchward, objecting that frizz was not germane. But the judge allowed Replogle to answer, the latter's own pate frizz rising to the occasion. He wasn't sure who had told this particular woman to defrizz. Apparently she had frizzed without his permission. There was more than one notable snicker from the gallery. I had to try very hard not to do the same. There would be plenty of embarrassing moments when my appearance and my sex would be degraded. It was hard, frankly, not to enjoy this one moment.

Other inconsistencies in Replogle's testimony included his statement that he and Ridge had carefully pondered my removal. The two of them had gone for a walk in the alley, relating their "gut-level" concern that the research was incorrect, that to remove me would be the wrong thing to do. They had "searched and personally searched a lot" but then decided they had no choice but to axe me. Supposedly this decision had been made the day before it had been acted upon. But Dennis was able to produce Replogle's handwritten notes on a document nearly a month prior which stated that I "didn't compare well to Anne Peterson in any image area," that I had pulled down Scott's popularity and that I was "out."

By far Replogle's most telling testimony picked up by every wire service and reporter was his response when asked what the most important criterion was in selecting a television news anchor. "If one had to rank them, I would put that (appearance) at the top of the list. I don't want to discount the other elements, but if one had to rank them, I would put that at the top of the list." If he had made his number one priority clear when first recruiting me from Santa Barbara, I never would have gone to Kansas City. I had put appearance way down on the list and had been extraordinarily clear on that fact.

One incident relating to Replogle's credibility revealed Judge Steven's attitude on the subject of admissibility of evidence. We had two witnesses who had been at an advertising club luncheon after my demotion, where Replogle had been the M.C. With his good buddy, president of ABC News, at his side, Replogle got up and addressed the group of five hundred. Perhaps expecting an appreciative chuckle, he offered, "If anyone needs an anchorwoman *real* cheap, I know where you can get one." Replogle denied having made the remark. Our witnesses swore that he had and that an unappreciative groan had gone through the audience when he had. Replogle could only remember that "to loosen up the audience and attempt to get a laugh, and in an ad-lib fashion—I don't recall the specific quote, but I did make a reference to the fact that there was an anchor available." Judge Stevens would not allow the definitive testimony of our two witnesses to be heard by the jury. It seems he took offense at one of the witnesses in deliberations in chambers. When asked how she happened to remember the specific words of Replogle's comments, Carolyn Copeland Henry, an advertising manager for the Davis Paint Company, testified, "Because I am a woman." Because Judge Stevens took umbrage at her woman-identified memory, the jury would not get to ascertain this incident.

It didn't take too much of an imaginative leap to wonder what other little sexist, insulting and blacklisting discussions Replogle and the network exec might have engaged in privately.

I hadn't filed this suit out of either naïveté, or expectation of using the notoriety to get another job. I suspected that if you speak out for too much integrity in a business which is supposed to embody the search for truth, you may never work again, or at least not for a long, long time. It was a painful recognition, one I had realized from the onset, yet something I had hoped would be reversible once the whole story was fully revealed.

Replogle left the stand to be greeted by the mystery woman, sporting a look that screamed "professional elegance." I could smell her perfume fifty yards away. She and his other attendants whisked Replogle out of the courtroom for the morning recess. I wondered if she had been the least bit troubled by his glib testimony that he had set a low budget "for a female anchor" when he first hired me, and that he had never considered paying the woman who replaced me with a salary comparable to the male in the same job? Didn't the mystery woman flinch just a little when Dennis had gotten Replogle to admit that Brenda Williams's education surpassed Scott Feldman's and that she had been at the station longer than he had, and had proven market acceptability? Yet Kent Replogle would never have considered giving her more than half Scott's pay. Someone, I don't remember which of our group, mentioned that they thought the mystery woman was a lawyer.

Another woman who like me had been deemed incapable of achieving the look of "professional elegance" demanded by the TV consultants, was due next to take the stand. But first, in chambers, Judge Stevens admonished Sarah that he would be watching like a hawk during her examination of the next witness, Pam Whiting. In his own words, "I am going to be very inflexible about her testifying to any opinions or conclusions or comparisons or any statements about discrimination. Are you putting her on?" Sarah firmly said yes and then raised an objection to his ruling. In essence, if Replogle's opinions had been freely allowed, then it would be prejudicial not to let Pam's opinions also be heard.

Pam Whiting was stopped frequently by Sandra Schermerhorn, with the judge sustaining nearly every objection. She managed, however, to describe how consultant Lynn Wilford had complained that one of Pam's eyes was smaller than the other and then had opined, "Appearance on air was more important for women than it was for men." Pam had not forgotten that remark. Having once worked as a radio news director, she knew what could and could not be stated to an employee under EEOC guidelines.

Pam also remembered Ridge telling her that Scott always looked good, but that it was even more important for

Christine and her to look good on the air. She told of Ridge's reprimand when she once raced her tail off to get a late-breaking story which was to be that night's lead, outclassing all the other competition in town. Afterwards, Ridge was concerned apparently only with what Pam looked like while she delivered the piece on the set. He told her that next time she should pay more attention to her appearance. Nary a peep was uttered about a well-done scoop. The height of the absurd came one night when Pam was ordered home after anchoring the early newscast to change clothes for the late broadcast. To some degree, that was not entirely out of the scope of a news director's authority, but in this case there were extenuating circumstances. The roads were virtually impassable due to a major blizzard. Pam recalled the dress she had been wearing as lavender and high-collared, and in no way bizarre, though it might not have been found in the pages of "Dress for Success," which Pam, like me, had been admonished to memorize.

Amidst flurries of objections, Pam managed to recount management's directives to give Scott the lead story rather than the female co-anchor. Judge Stevens allowed Pam to tell why she had refused to talk to Metromedia lawyers during the preparation for the trial. Pam described her employment as both painful and humiliating. She admitted that she hoped I would win the lawsuit, her bias freely displayed.

Summing up, Pam revealed what had prompted her to resign from Channel 9 to go back to a career in radio. She had found TV news, as practiced at Channel 9, pitifully superficial and grossly unfair in the types of pressures which were applied to the female broadcasters and not to the males.

Next on the stand was a man whose expensive advice had created many of the pressures on both Pam and me: defense witness Ed Bewley, president of the consulting company which had played such a pivotal role in the case. His firm's new name was Audience Research and Development. Earlier he had called it Media Associates. Unlike many of his key employees, he had actually studied journalism in college and had even been an anchorman in Columbus, Ohio. Elusive and well-dressed, Bewley was being paid $1,000 plus expenses per day for his attestations of truth. Despite no training in statistical analysis, he ran a business which featured attitude polling as its cornerstone. Audience Research was still being paid according to a contract it had with Metromedia and the new owners at KMBC, the Hearst Corporation, though the company had discontinued their services by the time of the trial. Bewley described part of his job as helping stations to "create news and other kinds of programming" to enable them to gain more audience. That description, delivered in an offhand manner, succinctly went to the root of the problem journalists face with consultants. These experts are trying to package news as a product. That is the antithesis to every honest reporter's fundamental goal. One cannot cross certain lines and still call a television program "news."

Apologist for a suspect practice, Bewley plied his dubious craft at TV stations all over the country. He gave advice and consent at five network-owned and operated stations, five CBS flagship stations. He was part and parcel of the scene at forty-five other stations, all of them network affiliates. His influence was staggering. Millions of people literally had their news information colored by the manipulations of this behind-the-scenes character. Bewley described two of his workers: Lynn Wilford, a "talent performance specialist," and Steve Meachum, head of research. Wilford still worked there. Meachum, the man who had called me a "mutt," had been "gradually phased out," according to Bewley.

Bewley spoke of the services his company had provided to KMBC. They had recommended the specialist system of reporting, naming a general assignment reporter as "medical specialist," "government specialist," or the like. The motivation was to convince the audience that these reporters had special expertise in such fields, even if they didn't. The essential need to create the illusion of credibility is a theme which runs through consultant theory, affecting not just clothing, makeup, and speech patterns. Media Associates had encouraged Channel 9 to hire a female nightly co-anchor because their research had indicated that more "warmth and comfort" was needed in the newscast. What they wanted was a bride for Scott Feldman. They had sent many tapes from their bloodbank to Channel 9 management, but no one either seemed right or was cheap enough—that is, until me. The problem was that no one had bothered to tell me that I was being hired to bring "warmth, teamwork, partnership and comfort" to the news program.

When Metromedia apparently perceived that I was not doing those things, they did not look to see what I *was* doing as a serious newscaster. Rather, they set out to test Kansas City's "negative" attitudes towards Christine Craft. Focus group questions and telephone surveys were designed to elicit nothing that was positive.

What a contrast this was to the way they had dealt with Scott Feldman when he tested out as "lukewarm" after just six months on the job! "Too early," they said, "that was to be expected." He hadn't been there long enough to really get a good specific sample. On the contrary, I was being torn to shreds by Steve Meachum, the consultant leader of a focus group, when I had barely been there six months. Meachum was quoted as having asked the questions management had helped write: "Let's be honest about this, is she a mutt? Let's spend ninety seconds destroying Christine Craft." When confronted with those lines in his deposition, Bewley said he had attended the focus group sessions, and stated as the moderator's boss that if Steve Meachum had made that kind of remark to some focus group respondents, he would have been fired by our company, "so I guarantee in every way possible Steve Meachum did not make that comment." When asked again in the trial, Bewley fumbled pathetically, saying he'd made the earlier comment "late in the day," and that now, on further reflection, he would have to "examine the context of the group...." After all, according to Bewley, a focus group is "an attempt...to get people to talk openly about their feelings on certain things. So the moderator has to, in some measure, become a part of the group dynamics, and in so doing may have to challenge somebody if they say something with a counter remark, or may inject levity into the circumstances if anger or emotion is developing in the group." Bewley admitted that he had no education in research or statistics beyond a possible undergraduate course he couldn't quite remember. He denied having heard the tapes even during the defendant's prepping of him for the trial. One wonders what they had talked about at lunch; he, Shannon, Replogle and counsel.

There were only a few restaurants in close proximity to the courthouse. All of us crossed each other's paths each day in the sweltering streets on the way to and from lunch. Judge Stevens's frequent lunch partner during the trial was an eighth circuit appellate judge, another Reagan appointee, John R. Gibson. They favored the masculine ambiance of the Kansas City Club.

I must admit, it had been delightful to see Bewley squirm. I'd seen how consultants could make money by recommending change. Even if their changes didn't work, they still were paid fabulous amounts to strut their pseudo-professional advice. At Channel 9, all their concepts had failed: specialist reporters, on-air unanchored promotions, Scott Feldman as a "close-up" reporter, Christine Craft as a bearer of warmth and cuddliness. Bewley found himself a little more naked than he ever wanted to be, especially in front of so many people. Perhaps he should start a new consultant's seminar: "How to look your credible best in a very bad light."

After the air cleared, Scott Feldman, the final witness of the first week of the trial, was to be sworn in. During a recess for a moment in the hallway we had a chance to speak to each other for the first time since my going-away party back in August, 1981. "How's your dog?" I asked him. More than anything else in our relationship, we shared a love of dogs. I knew his three-legged black female lab was the main love of his life, along with his wife Janet, of course. Scott told me the sad tale of his dog's demise. I, in turn, told him of mine. We didn't say anything else, we didn't need to. I knew it was strange for either of us to be here. I wanted to have confidence that he would tell the truth. But all I could be sure of was that he would testify very carefully. After all, he was still the Metromedia anchorman.

Wisely, not volunteering anything he wasn't asked, Scott rowed a steady course through details of our time together. He had thought my attire was a bit casual for the audition, but did think I looked nice, anyway. He testified he hadn't heard any comments from anyone that day suggesting that the way I was presenting myself would be unacceptable at KMBC.

He told of our mutual dislike of the "expertise" of Lynn Wilford, and of her rape of his favorite poem, "The Raven," during one of our coaching threesomes. However, considerably less punchy than he had been in depositions, Scott had to be reminded of his statement that "Christine throughout had expressed to me she was unhappy about the way they were trying to make her over, initially from the outset."

Then in a litany of no's Scott certified that he'd never been required to follow a clothing calendar, nor had he ever taken any directives on appearance changes from either management or consultants. He contrasted his treatment with what he saw as their attempts to change my look. He'd seen me in the "unusual, theatrical, heavily made up around the eyes, mouth" makeup that Lynn Wilford had so artlessly applied. Under all that glop was, in his opinion, a conscientious and hard-working co-anchor.

When it came to the really big question, what Ridge had told him were the reasons for my demotion that August day two years before, Scott was in the hot seat. In court, he declared he couldn't *remember* if Mr. Shannon had told him "the public perceived Christine Craft was too old, too unattractive, and did not defer to men." However, Dennis remembered his saying something quite different in his deposition.

With Giffin furiously protesting every question leading up to the inevitable reading of Scott's earlier testimony, Judge Stevens had perhaps his fairest moment. At the bench, Dennis held his own against Giffin. "This is key, key, key testimony, underline it four times." The judge himself now read Scott's deposition for the first time and declared his surprise. The evidence was allowed and the deposition read as follows: "Ridge had said, because research came out very poorly and that never in the history of Metromedia research had anyone tested so poorly, and I found that hard to believe. I said that is astounding. She holds that kind of—I mean, what could be so wrong? He expressed to me some of the things the research said...that she didn't—that the public perceived she didn't defer to men, that she was—appeared too old or too unattractive, things of that nature." Scott admitted he'd given the earlier answer, but did not care to elaborate.

It was a compelling bit of testimony from which the jury would have to draw its own conclusions about truth and coercion. As the week drew to a close, we had presented evidence which corroborated my claims. The week to come would include the rest of our case and all of theirs.

I knew we had done well, and I felt not the slightest reservation about either Dennis or Sarah. They were making a thoroughly well-prepared presentation of the facts that had driven me in the first place to seek a jury's decision. Sarah was gaining trial experience in one of the most publicized legal events of the year. Dennis was proving to be the Kansas City slugger, never losing the passion or the ethics of our argument, winning, I felt, every round.

Replogle's patronizing manner, the consultant's glibness, Pam's painful honesty, and Scott's halting corroboration of key evidence—all this could not have gone unnoticed by the jury. Also, they had seen my colleagues attest to the sex discrimination that I had told them of at Channel 9. It can be very hard to prove the fact of the matter, if you have to depend on people who by testifying may be risking their livelihood. In this case, my co-worker's testimony would serve to vindicate me. I knew, as I always had, that we would win, no matter how humiliating the defense case became in the week to follow.

Back at Marty's, up to my elbows in Woolite, I planned my courtroom fashion calendar for the week ahead. Perhaps I would try switching things around, the skirt with a different top, the top with a different bottom. After all, many would be watching to see how I'd look when the defense case took the spotlight, many, including the mystery woman who always seemed to take particular interest in my clothes.

6.

LAPSED CATHOLICS THAT we were, Dennis and I made a qualified promise to our mutual God. We might not make it to Mass every Sunday thereafter, but we would sure be bending knees for the next two weekends. Though both of us lamented the loss of the Latin Mass of our youth, going to church with his family fortified us both with a shared belief and prayer: "Oh Lord, this jury must see the strength of our argument."

Drawing sustenance, too, from all the letters I had received by this time, I reread parts of the ones that meant the most. One man had written to the *Kansas City Times:* "Dear Editor: After reading in the paper of Christine Craft's being fired for not being a glamour girl, let me say that when I first saw her on TV I couldn't believe my eyes. Here at last was a girl who wasn't a glamour puss fashion plate. Christine was just Christine. I didn't feel embarrassed watching the news because I was watching with the clothes I had worked in and been in all day."

And another addressed to Ridge Shannon and copied to me: "I am a female between 26 and 49 and I know several other young women in the K.C. area who feel as I do: Christine Craft was about the only good thing you had going for you on 'The News.' If you base any kind of opinion on looks, how in the world would people like that Replogle fellow ever be allowed on the screen for any purpose? I am going to have to go either to Channel 4 or 5 for my six o'clock news in the future. I don't know where you get your so-called experts, but they don't have a pulse on what the real feeling is out in the community. I think I can tell you more about what people feel about your program than the Dallas consultants. I work in a local government office and everyone I've talked to (and I've talked to many people) agree that Christine Craft got a bum rap. I can only hope she finds this bad experience to be a stepping stone to bigger and better things because I, for one, will be rooting for her."

I polished that off with some sweet words from Bill Luton Senior, patriarchal owner of the Santa Barbara station: "Chris, I am so glad they did not think you glamourous—I heartily disagree! Really you are quite nice and we all love you. Their loss is our gain. Bill L."

Crusty rich old Republican cowboy that he was, Luton had once told me, "I'm no feminist, but I hope you kick their butts!" It had been a nice, nice thing for him to say and I planned not to disappoint. I could imagine the steel and sparkle of his eyes as I wound my psyche up for another week of trial.

The other side was doing its best at damage control. Denying that they were "posturing" or practicing "tokenism," KMBC announced it had just hired a woman to broadcast its sports news. When reached in Columbus, Ohio, sportscaster Karen Kornacki offered her opinion that current events had opened the doors for other women at KMBC.

Dan Rather on the "CBS Evening News" called the case "far-reaching," and Op-Ed pages in everything from *USA Today* to the *Washington Post* were becoming keen on the subject, some questioning my naïveté in expecting TV news to be something different from entertainment.

Good cartoons poured forth from the nation's greatest quills. Don Wright in the *Miami Herald* drew an anchor couple inside a screen:

> "Good evening. I'd like to welcome our new anchorperson here at Eyeball News, Ms. Darlene Dabney. She replaces our former anchorperson, Katrina Faloo."
> "Thank you, Biff!"
> "Things are really heating up in South America as

communist guerillas in El Saladora blow up another bridge! We'll have details in a moment, eh Darlene?"

"Actually, that's El Salvador, Biff, not Saladora and it's located in Central America, not South America. Also, many of the guerillas are not communists at all!"

(Silently): "God, She's ugly."

Since we knew audio tapes would be played and would take aim at my appearance, it was important that we present our own witness to question whether the focus group "research" was really reliable. Our expert witness was an associate professor of Communications Studies at the University of Kansas. Dr. Thomas Beisecker's work included extensive experience in the design of statistical research. Unlike many "experts" called in trials with great regularity, Tom Beisecker had never testified in a trial before. We had asked him to read the Media Associates reports, listen to the focus groups' tapes, and determine from his review whether or not the conclusions were defensible.

Beisecker wasted no time in pointing out his observations of the tapes. For starters, he stated that he felt like he was "listening to backyard gossip," not research. From what he had heard, he could not draw *any* defensible conclusions.

He suggested the shortcomings of focus groups themselves. The sample is small, reflecting the opinion of the loudest respondent, and also subject to the attitude of the moderator himself.

At the particular sessions in question, a dozen people, chosen by sex and age, would be taken from the shopping center, given $25 each, cookies and soft drinks and put before one-way glass. Behind the glass sat R. Kent Replogle, Ridge Shannon, and other Metromedia executives. The people were told they were being audio-taped. No mention was made of their also being carefully watched. Steve Meachum, the Media Associates moderator, would set up his group, saying by way of introduction either... "This is your chance to get rid of the things you don't like to see on the news," or to a group of men, "This is your chance to do more than just yell at the TV. You can speak up and say I really hate that guy or I really like that broad." To another group of men, he suggested: "This is your chance to unload on these sons of bitches who make $100,000 a year."

One group of women between the ages of twenty-five and thirty-five was by far the toughest on me. Meachum made the following statement to this group: "Let's spend thirty seconds destroying Christine Craft." To a group of men he chose to say, "Is she a mutt? Let's be honest about this."

Beisecker demonstrated easily why he felt such statements in themselves evidenced bias and would further influence any reactions that group members might have.

Even accounting for Meachum's deplorable techniques, it was true that the collection of younger women for the most part were not fond of me. One housewife complained that I seemed to be a cynical, hard woman. However, another woman said she thought I had a very professional speaking voice. Her opinion was drowned out by the naysayers, Meachum making no attempt to elaborate on the positive feature she had brought up.

When they discussed the male anchors, Meachum asked the women if they wanted one particularly handsome anchor's phone number. When one of the women noted that this handsome anchor had a handicap from childhood polio, Meachum told everyone not to waste their sympathies on someone who made $100,000 a year. Not only was that remark staggeringly insensitive, it was totally inaccurate. The anchor in question made considerably less money. No one on the air in Kansas City made that much in 1981.

When a man in one of the groups waxed adoringly over Anne Peterson's "cuteness," Meachum popped right in and said to the others, "Jim just wants sex with Anne Peterson."

Beisecker indicated that when a group of men was first asked about Channel 9, there were no comments about me at all until Meachum initiated them. These men described me as a new person—they hadn't seen enough of me to have formed an opinion. Meachum persisted, making them compare me to Anne Peterson.

Finally, one said I wasn't as flashy. Meachum leaped on that, turning it into the assertion that I wasn't flashy enough to do the news. When one man expressed the view that I was more aggressive with the actual stories than the other women in town, Meachum again didn't try to develop that positive analysis.

Beisecker illustrated over and over how Meachum appeared to place certain of the female anchors either in a comparatively advantageous or disadvantageous position. I was never placed in the former category.

The professor went on to show that the focus groups had been conducted inconsistently. There was no standardized research procedure. A group of women would not be shown videotapes of Christine Craft and Anne Peterson; yet a group of men would be. Cynthia Smith was not shown at all, to anyone. If this was supposed to be a survey of how the audience looked at the three anchorwomen in town, it was a strange way to do it.

Beisecker moved on to describe the larger phone survey of some four hundred people, one that was designed according to the results of the earlier groups. With a wry expression, he noted that people over sixty-four or under eighteen were apparently less valuable consumers of news product, since they were excluded from the survey. I had always thought we were doing the news for everyone.

In a profound opening paragraph of its survey conclusions, Media Associates had declared: "The addition of Christine Craft to the KMBC anchor team is not positively accepted by viewers and is the primary force driving them to the Anne Peterson-Wendall Anschutz pairing on Channel 5."

Beisecker picked that statement to shreds, asking why no one changed their viewing habits during my tenure, whether my presence had motivated them to turn to Channel 5, or, finally whether they were indeed watching Channel 5 instead of 9. Without eliciting answers to those specific questions, it was legitimately impossible to conclude as Media Associates had.

Beisecker methodically demonstrated without question that Media Associates' survey techniques were biased, unstandardized, and inaccurate. In addition, the language of the focus groups was coarse and sexist.

There was, of course, no way of knowing if the jury agreed, but it seemed impossible that they could have failed to see the research to some degree for what it was.

Cross-examination under Mark Johnson's bobbing Adam's apple zeroed in on the quickly admitted fact that Tom Beisecker's expertise was not in researching TV news audiences. But Beisecker hung tough; he stated that a rigorous method of collecting and analyzing data must be utilized by any study that calls itself "research."

Johnson attempted to characterize the research as valid merely because it had been expensive and of a type used industry-wide. Beisecker's professorial disdain for that stance stayed intact throughout the counter-questioning.

The end of our case drew closer. Providing some less weighty moments after all the statistical testimony was Sherry Chastain, a woman who had been a news producer at Channel 9 before my arrival. Sherry had worked for both Ridge Shannon and Kent Replogle and without hesitation she described how appearance had always been the most important thing at the Metromedia station. She said Ridge had instructed her to monitor the appearance of female anchors and reporters, but never males. He had flown into a fit when one woman had worn her hair pulled back for a newscast, complaining that she looked like a "frumpy housewife." He observed of the same woman that he hoped she wouldn't turn sideways because she had "a big honker." The male counterpart of that particular anchor team was bald, with a bad toupée and thick glasses, yet nothing was ever said about monitoring his appearance.

Before they ever sought to hire me, KMBC's practice of hounding its women on-air employees about appearance had been long established. Sherry Chastain was not allowed by Judge Stevens to testify that, as a Channel 9 news producer, she had been paid considerably less than the male producers for the same job.

It was fine consolation to know that Sherry later went on to use that particular fiscal experience as one inspiration for her best-selling non-fiction book *Winning the Salary Negotiation Game*.

Our last witness was Brenda Williams, the woman who had replaced me as Channel 9's co-anchor. A handsome black woman my age, Brenda had never tried to be particularly friendly to me. I'm sure she resented the fact that Metromedia had treated her poorly throughout the years and had brought me in from out of town to take the job she felt should have been offered to her. Since we had no personal bond, I had no idea what the tone and substance of her testimony would be. Once on the stand, she was matter-of-fact but specific. I only wish Judge Stevens had let the jury hear the most powerful part of what she had to say.

What they did hear bore potent enough witness to Metromedia's style of paying women anchors less than they paid men. After my forced departure, Brenda was originally told she could fill in as co-anchor until they found someone they liked better. After the station came under scrutiny because of my allegations, they did the least assailable thing. They offered the job to Brenda permanently if she could agree to salary conditions.

She asked for comparable pay to Scott Feldman's, in view of the fact that she'd been at the station longer than Scott, and had won several Missouri press awards. Nonetheless, they flat out told her they had no intention of offering her a salary equal to Scott's. Brenda's request for *comparable* pay was nowhere in the ball park of what they had in mind for her. They told her to ask for what I had been making, which by that time was approximately half of Scott Feldman's pay. Brenda eventually signed a starting contract for $2,500 more per year than I had received.

The defense objected strenuously, with Judge Stevens sustaining several of those objections, when Brenda began to get into the meaty details of her relationship with KMBC. By way of proof, Sarah asked several revealing questions after the judge had ordered the jury removed from the courtroom. At that point, Brenda became dynamically descriptive. Ridge Shannon had told her again and again that she was applying for the same job I had, and therefore should get the same salary. It mattered little to them that she was a home-town person, that she had won more awards than Scott, that she had more academic broadcast credentials than either of us. Finally she had settled for the puny remuneration, knowing it was unfair. The station had told her if she didn't take it, they had some woman in Springfield, Missouri who would, and for only $28,500. Brenda added: "My honest feelings are that the managers at that station had created a position for a woman, and a female co-anchor was only going to get so much money. I mean it was going to be substantially less than the male anchor."

Sarah argued that the specific testimony was crucial to our case. And though Judge Stevens at first seemed inclined to let the jury hear it, he changed his mind in mid-stream and decided they could hear only the question about whether reference had been made to me in Brenda Williams's negotiations for her job.

After only a partial line of inquiry, the witness was excused. Brenda was under obvious pressure, since she was still working for Replogle. On the stand she was like two different people, her passion and anger showing only when the jury was absent. I couldn't totally begrudge her position: she left the courthouse and went back to deliver her share of the six o'clock newscast with Scott Feldman at her side.

We wrapped up our case with readings from the depositions of Lynn Wilford, my former very own personal TV consultant.

Wilford hadn't made it to the trial. Since she lived out of judicial range, we had no way to subpoena her as our witness, and Metromedia apparently had no desire to see her allied to their side in front of a jury.

Her deposition revealed that Media Associates personnel had made negative comments about my appearance even on the original audition tape with Scott. Apparently they found my cashmere sweater too casual and the back of my head too unkempt. Lynn Wilford had also concluded before even meeting me that my appearance "wouldn't work in Kansas City" because I wasn't "conservative" enough. Lynn based this opinion on passages in the "Dress for Success" book which posits that in the Midwest dress must be conservative.

She also had discussed with Ridge my "problems on camera" over the phone. She remembered Ridge telling her not to work with me on appearance, "only to talk a bit about dress, and not to work on makeup or hair" while I was in Dallas. He told Lynn he wanted to work on that himself in Kansas City. This was all occurring at the time Metromedia was telling me they liked my appearance and wouldn't want to change a thing.

The presentation of our case was completed. Giffin asked Stevens to dismiss the fraud portion of the case, essentially because I had made more money at KMBC than I had at KEYT. Stevens refused to do that, reminding everyone that he'd reserve his powers for perhaps another, more appropriate time.

Now it was the defense turn to make a case, and starting off with more of a clang than a bang, Metromedia set in motion its parade of evidence.

Here came Maureen Shauvers teetering along on black ankle-wrapped spike heels. As the Macy's fashion consultant clicked her way to the stand, behind her a solemn group completed the processional. Giffin's aides rolled in a noisy metal clothing rack on wheels, hung with the items from my fashion calendar. "Oh my god, it's the clothes," I uttered under my breath, barely able to repress a roar of laughter. Maureen kept me sober. Dressed in a black sheath outfit, she had only a slash of reddest lipstick to provide a note of contrast. Maybe she'd thought it was going to be a funeral.

In barely audible tones, she characterized our first meeting as one where I had sought her out, asking her if I could have free clothing. Even Ridge Shannon would later testify that he had introduced the two of us. As this whopper emitted from her clenched jaw past the lipstick smudged teeth, I knew we were in for some doozies. Thank God, at least she told her version of the truth very ineptly.

According to Maureen, Macy's had made her work for me on her lunch hours. Unfed, she'd had to put up with my absolute ideas of what I did and didn't like. Imperious sort that I was, I disliked everything feminine with frills or lace. And of course, no matter how poor Maureen had slaved, I had the final word on what was chosen.

On the other hand, strangely enough, Maureen swore I didn't have any interest in clothes at all, and she was obliged to design a fashion calendar for me, prepared on her vacation time.

Ms. Schermerhorn conducted the direct examination. She had Maureen rise and address the clothing rack, giving the prices for various garments. Maureen went through it all, pointedly stating that to her count, there were about twelve pieces missing. She didn't know where they were.

Ms. Schermerhorn looked intrigued and pressed onward. What did the twelve pieces consist of? Why silk blouses and silk skirts, of course. You'd think someone with bad taste like mine at least would have pilfered the polyester.

I grew restless waiting for Dennis to have his chance.

Coolly, with surgical precision, Dennis dissected the body of impressions that Maureen had attempted to leave behind her. "Was she implying that I had taken silk clothing?"

Actually, as it turned out, this guardian of the supposedly purloined hadn't really *seen* the clothes since before I left two years ago. She had no idea, she said, where they had been in the interim or why she had been asked to check the clothing rack against her original documents just that very morning, and had discovered the suspicious shortage.

Concerning the free, on-her-own-time work that she had done for the talent at KMBC, Dennis forced her to reveal that she'd been on the Macy's payroll all along. Pathetically dismissed without playing a part you'd want to be remembered for, she click-clopped out of the courtroom, the rack dragged out clanging behind her. Her choice to wear a black sheath had been perfect though. She'd been dressed right all along, for her own mini-funeral.

To polish the tarnished image of research, Metromedia next called Thomas Wiese, the man whose company had run the telephone survey of Kansas City TV viewers. He remembered having taken a few courses in statistics many years ago. Dennis pointed out that Wiese's part in the research had nothing to do with the design of the questions or the ultimate conclusions drawn from the raw data. His description of data gathering was sheerly technical, and his testimony had little relevance to the case.

Equally monotonous was the testimony of Metromedia's third witness, the man whose Connecticut company provided population samples for the survey. I guess the defendant's purpose was to imply that these techniques were highly efficient and unbiased. They probably were, but this company, too, had nothing to do with the design or conclusions of the study.

Next on the stand was the woman from the shopping center mall company that had sought out and paid the focus group respondents. She testified to the female hostess service, the cokes and coffee and money given to focus group participants, and to the clients behind the 4' by 7' one-way mirror. It was interesting to note that if you were someone with the wrong age or sex, Metromedia wasn't interested in what you had to say in a focus group about the news.

Maybe it was just my bias, but I couldn't see how Metromedia's case had been helped by their presentation of the first four witnesses. Up next was someone a little more interesting.

Robert K. King, a man who had never graduated from college, had nonetheless had a long and varied career in both radio and television, having managed several ABC stations ranging in size from miniscule to major. He had worked for twenty-one years in a wide variety of executive positions for Capital Cities Communications, a powerful broadcast conglomerate which owned many TV and radio stations as well as the *Kansas City Times* and *Star*. He'd also been chairman of the board of the ABC television affiliate association. King had lectured broadcasters nationwide on such subjects as "talents" and "news portrayal," having resigned from those prestigious positions to start his own consulting firm.

He testified to the wide use of consultants and research in the news business, a practice established not to enhance the integrity of news, but rather to reach more potential product consumers for advertisers.

By far the most interesting part of King's testimony was his description of pay differentials for anchor talent doing the same job: When determining what to pay people, you considered not only their background, but also how much you wanted them. In Mr. King's words, "It's a little like how much is Kareem Abdul-Jabbar worth to the next team that gets his services. It's a matter of negotiations."

I'm sure the jury had to stretch a little to see any similarities between me and Kareem. However, such factors for Mr. King and others like him apparently took slam-dunk precedence over equal pay laws.

Under cross-examination Mr. King acknowledged that he was a reasonably good friend of John Kluge, chairman of the board of Metromedia. He was friendly with Robert Bennett, senior vice-president of Metromedia, and a twenty-year friend of Tom Dougherty, Metromedia's Washington legal counsel. King had known Kent Replogle for at least ten years. He denied having talked with any of them about this case, except with Mr. Bennett in a three-minute phone conversation when he had been asked to be an expert witness.

Dennis pointed out to Mr. King some facts he may not have known. My background had included less formal broadcast academic training than Scott Feldman, but I had a college degree and had shot, edited, and produced for several years. I had network experience and Scott did not. I had worked in San Francisco, a much larger market than Scott had ever worked in. Apparently King was under the impression that I had been a noontime or weekend anchor in Santa Barbara, an experience he said was worth less in his earlier testimony than weeknight anchoring. In fact, there had never been a noontime newscast in Santa Barbara. I had co-anchored the late evening weeknight news. Someone had the facts wrong. The big corporate executive had to admit that it was difficult to compare two people vis-à-vis salary when he didn't know the full extent of their comparative backgrounds.

Dennis made an impressive point that Mr. King's livelihood depended on the use of consultants by television stations. Of course, he would be their champion, even though he admitted that all one needed to be a television consultant was to hang out a shingle. Neither experience nor credentials were required. No more testimony was required from Mr. King after he acknowledged that he had no degree in statistics and that he hadn't looked at the research done on me to see if it had been conducted accurately. We finished for the day, only three more remained.

The weather was stifling even in the early evening. A multitude of cameras still recorded our every arrival and leave-taking. Dennis and Sarah and Carole and Pat and I found a Holiday Inn with a cool bar where we quaffed a few beers and toasted ourselves to a job well done...so far. Tomorrow would continue in earnest the no doubt well-financed effort by Metromedia. Their list of witnesses was a mile long and it included many big names in broadcast news, particularly ABC management figures. Would they call in the other elephant guns to destroy the mousey aging anchorette? Or would they be careful to avoid too much of the David and Goliath scenario, suspecting it could backfire in the end? We swallowed a few more toasts, glad to have gotten away from it all, at least for a little while. Over the bar, the six o'clock news theme music came blaring out..."THIS IS THE NEWS." The lead story as delivered by Scott Feldman and Brenda Williams was none other than the latest machinations in the Craft case.

The next day provided some considerable volatility. Steve Meachum, the man who had called me a mutt, took the stand. I didn't recall ever seeing him before, but when I did, I wondered if he'd looked in the mirror lately. Bespectacled, balding, with premature double chins, Mr. Meachum was hardly a handsome man. A droopy walrus mustache hid, God knew, what multitude of errors. Ordinarily, I couldn't care less what people look like. But during this trial I had, shall we say, a heightened aesthetic sensibility.

In his early examination of Meachum, when Giffin decided to play a tape compilation of all the references to me in the focus groups, I quietly let my own protective instincts become visible. I rose from my chair at the plaintiff's table and left the courtroom. I had no desire to hear the taped insults from unseen people as others watched for my reactions.

I heard later how Meachum had justified his use of derogatory remarks about me. He had called me a "mutt" because he believed a moderator has to make people feel comfortable enough to say what they are really thinking. He had used, he said, "the kind of terminology that men use in discussions about women."

Carefully prepared, he went through his presentation of how the research had been conducted and processed and how conclusions had been drawn. He strayed frequently from the proper question and answer format, causing Dennis to interrupt and object. The judge seemed to have only the mildest propensity to hold Giffin and Meachum to standard procedure.

However, under the less accommodating requirement of answering Dennis's questions, Meachum was infinitely less self-assured. At first he balked aggressively when Dennis caught him in inconsistencies between deposition and trial statements. He had, well he hadn't, well really he had conducted focus groups before coming to Media Associates. He hadn't, well he might have, well he couldn't lie because it was being read to him that he had done such and such. He began to look slightly green at the gills.

It turned out that Meachum in the past had done research for Channel 9 while working for another company. In those earlier studies, he ruled that he didn't have enough information after six months to evaluate the market status of such short-time performers as Scott Feldman, or the newly hired Anne Peterson. In sharp contrast, with Christine Craft, six months had been more than ample to make absolute judgments.

The emerging picture of Steve Meachum was less than flattering. This marketing "expert" had taken only one college course in statistics, a class he admitted was purely introductory.

Dennis reminded him that one of the ways he got a focus group to open up about anchorpeople was to suggest "... maybe we could construct a hate list and...you know, snuff them."

Meachum prided himself on being a master of the regional vernacular, the kind of guy who knew how to elicit a negative response from just about anyone! Just give him a roomful of midwestern blue-collars and see what he could do.

Regarding the resentment in his groups he created by wrongfully stating that various anchorpeople made $100,000 a year, he justified himself with the statement, "The point is, they make a lot of money and a hundred thousand dollars is a figure that you can banter around in pretty secure knowledge that you are not specifically identifying one individual's exact level of salary." I guess the expert didn't know that no TV person in Kansas City was making $100,000 a year. The women each made considerably less than half.

Asking the guys if they wanted to sleep with another woman anchor was just Meachum's "brand of humor." When Dennis suggested that such an opening to a focus group might impact the way participants viewed women from then on, Judge Stevens called the question "far afield." Dennis may have struck a nerve very close to home. After all, Meachum had made the men grade Anne Peterson and me on a scale of one to ten.

Meachum's testimony was turning out to be the most fascinating and unsavory of all, a real look at a business with the most dubious sort of credibility.

The man claimed he probed both negative and positive attitudes. Yet nowhere in the phone survey was there a question about my strongest focus group point—my good speaking voice. Meachum had omitted it because according to him, everybody on the air has a good speaking voice.

At Media Associates, groups of people over sixty-four were never asked their opinions about local news because, as Meachum offered, "They are neither particularly influenceable [consultant speak] when you are attempting to attract an audience, nor are they willing to make strong comments on most things." Never mind that adults of all ages needed information to make good decisions regarding their communities. If they were over sixty-four, to the consultants they just didn't exist.

Dennis plowed through Meachum's techniques and left no stone unturned. When he reached the end, he asked Meachum: If Craft's negatives were pulling everyone down and turning all the viewers off, was it his position that Channel 9 was not the third-place station in the race?

No, as a matter of fact, Meachum had concluded in his report that "KMBC had narrowly increased its lead as the station most watched for local news." This was in comparison to his study of the year before Craft was hurting the hell out of them. The facts were something else. Even the twenty-five to thirty-four year olds who supposedly despised the sight of me watched Channel 9's news more than any other station.

Giffin's final questions merely rehashed the rationale for the bad research, as if by repeating it over and over again with an air of authority, it would gain the illusion of credibility. But that tack did not prevent Meachum leaving the stand somewhat diminished in stature. It must have been all that sitting.

Ending the third day of the second week, Sandra Schermerhorn took the part of Lynn Wilford in reading from the deposition detailing what her job as talent coach really meant: "making communicators communicate," "giving people permission to be themselves on camera," and other such pap.

I felt dyspeptic and went for a refreshing swim when the day ended. The Kansas City Athletic Club still had its pool in the middle of downtown. The building was being renovated and I made my way through a labyrinth of crumbling drywall finally to the interior waters of the Continental Hotel. There wasn't anyone there as I took my evening dip, from which I emerged refreshed as usual, giving a muttish bark or two for effect. Only two more days of this grueling ordeal remained. Swimming helped keep me emotionally stable. It was a world disconnected from the courtroom insults. If I was going to emerge from this mess with my psyche intact, I had to adopt a sort of distance, a numbness not unlike the attitude reporters assume when covering disasters. Swimming always helped me to achieve a healthy distance from unpleasant realities.

The final witness still to be called was Ridge Shannon. With his daughters and wife gazing on adoringly, Ridge took the stand and Giffin guided him through a recitation of the prodigious enormity of his broadcast experience.

He then told how he and Replogle had spent a sleepless night agonizing over whether or not to remove me from the anchor desk after they had seen the consultant research.

Shannon gave his account of how he had implemented their final decision. He said he had told me in his office that the research showed people were unable to hear me communicate because of my makeup, clothes, and stuttering delivery. Since I have never stuttered in my life and since Metromedia had no evidence of such alleged stuttering, I found at least this part absolutely ludicrous.

I glanced out into the courtroom and noticed that while the Shannon daughters had their heads down, the mother's head was raised heavenward, her eyes closed as if in silent prayer.

Her husband continued. According to him, I had called the audience unsophisticated. As I remembered it, he had said "the people of Kansas City are even more provincial than we had thought." He denied ever having mentioned age. He denied ever having mentioned deference to me. He said instead that he told me the viewers thought I was a buttinski.

Shannon's testimony regarding our entire relationship was peppered with subtle wordings of every critical point, in such a way that he would always appear to be the concerned, compassionate news director. He described himself as not just a news director, but "a rabbi, a counselor, a father confessor." Through all of this, the wife remained in her beatified state just behind the railing. Her husband, the priest, was giving witness.

He said that I told him I sometimes didn't wear makeup to do the news. (Never in my life have I either said that or done that. I may not pile it on, but I have always worn the standard combo of foundation, blush, mascara, eyeliner, lipstick.) He said I had begged Metromedia for help with makeup and clothes. (I distinctly recalled asking them *not* to hire me if they wanted to change my appearance.)

On the subject of the newspaper ads that had described me as "fresh from an anchor desk in California," Shannon denied that I had been promoted as coming from somewhere else.

In general, though, Ridge's testimony was the most powerful tool Metromedia had. They had saved their best witness for last. He seemed like such a nice guy, his account of events pretty much the same as mine. Most of the differences were subtle digs made in a low-key style. The only time he became emphatic was in the discussion of the events of August 14, 1981. He hadn't said any of the things I had attributed to him! He had genuinely liked me, after all. I couldn't help remembering some of his earlier testimony about his army service as a specialist in psychological warfare and propaganda.

Was I just imagining that the wife's lids fluttered and her lips began forming silent prayers, as Dennis began his own line of questioning? Not quite so fast, Mr. Shannon, not quite so fast.

First there was the matter that he had sat in court throughout the trial as a representative of Metromedia. He was no longer at Channel 9, just serving because he "felt he owed it to Metromedia." Supposedly there was no remuneration being paid to this currently unemployed man.

He had heard every witness. He was giving his testimony with an advantage no one else had. Could he tailor his answers carefully enough to avoid any of the hazards that had already been seen to be issues in this trial? He had the hardest task, but the biggest advantage.

Concerning a bar graph showing Scott and Christine's relative background in TV news, Mr. Shannon was asked if years spent reporting, shooting, editing, and on-air at a network had any weight at all in such evaluations. He had to admit that those factors of my experience had been omitted in the comparison.

Dennis continued his drilling, this time about the "fresh from California" ads. We produced the ad in all its glory, not even blown up, just life-sized. The jury read along with Dennis: "A new look at the news, Christine Craft joins Scott Feldman in reporting the news. Coming from an anchor position in California and a background of CBS network reporting, Christine is a new pro on Kansas City's professional news team."

Ridge at first said he had nothing to do with making those ads. Then later, well perhaps he had provided information to the production department so that *they* could write the ads. Just one little slip of paper. Oh well, it was "just advertising or promotion."

Remember, Christine Craft was the woman who was so inexperienced Metromedia couldn't pay her what her male counterpart made or even what he had made when he'd first started green to the area three years before.

It was after five o'clock, the usual quitting time, when Ridge stumbled over some dates and had about an hour's worth of questions before finishing. Recessed for that day, there was only one more left. I could barely sleep in anticipation of the final session.

The rest of Ridge resumed at 9 A.M. The courtroom was packed. Closing arguments were expected. Today would be the last chance for either side to make its points.

Dennis pulled out some business records from the first month of my tenure. Ridge had written in his monthly report that "The co-anchors had been viewed and it was working smoothly." This seemed to belie his testimony that they had major problems with me all through that first month. Ridge argued that his remarks were intended for public record and therefore emphasized the positive more than the negative. So much so that he had been forced to write in the same monthly report, "Word off the street indicates good acceptance of Christine Craft as Scott Feldman's partner. Time and ratings will tell." But Ridge Shannon and Kent Replogle had given me neither time nor ratings to prove I could succeed.

On another critical point Dennis reminded Ridge of his audition comments to me about Anne Peterson, whom he perceived to be anathema to journalism. Then they had turned around and removed me when people failed to perceive me as Anne Petersonish enough.

When the defense rested its case, Dennis was able to call me to the stand for some rebuttal clarification testimony.

Giffin and the judge balked at having me on the stand as the last person, but Dennis had every right to do so.

Giffin's closing arguments were true to form and contained no surprises. My claims were "unreasonable and outlandish." He defended Metromedia's prerogatives to control every aspect of my "performance." He defended the research as having "all the appearances of good research." He defended Metromedia's practice of paying at least two women anchors less than the man, because supposedly Scott Feldman had "obtained satisfaction from the viewing audience." Giffin pounced on my relationship with the supposedly Svengali-like Bob Hamilton. "Was Ms. Craft run off the job by Mr. Shannon, or did she walk off?" he asked. He implied that I was a mindless blob urged by the fiendish Bob into making a *cause célèbre* out of nothing.

Dennis kept it simple. I hadn't set out to be Joan of Arc, my lawsuit had been "born out of grave injustice." He took aim at the research. "What you have here is a sham." He reminded the jury that "if you send Christine packing, the defendant will do it again."

"If trust is meaningless, if equality (of pay) is ludicrous as Mr. Replogle said, by all means bring back a verdict for the defendant. That's fine. But if there is such a thing as justice, if there is something to be gained by standing up for your rights when they have been violated, then we urge you, please, to bring back a verdict for the plaintiff on all counts. And we will await your verdict."

Huge hot tears welled up in my eyes. My carefully conceived emotional distance began to crumble. I kept my face down, out of the sight of the jury.

It was close to the end of the day after they heard the instructions delivered by the court, and the lengthy harangue of both sides about the specifics of those instructions. I wasn't hearing anything more. Dennis's closing argument had crystalized all the reasons why I had sued. He had understood everything on every level. I could not have asked for a more brilliant summary.

The jury opted to return for continued deliberations on Monday and we had an anxious weekend to get through. Good humored diversion was provided by a huge picnic out at Sarah's house in the country. Everyone involved in our case brought their families and we talked very little about the trial. These people went out of their way to give me a sense of belonging and community. They knew I had some understandable rejection anxieties about Kansas City.

Marty and I, sitting at the breakfast table on Sunday morning, began to chuckle as we read together a feature article in the *Star*'s "Look" section. The article was entitled, "Looking Good, what they're wearing ... courtroom appearance of Christine Craft on trial too."

As we read, we kept waiting for the thing to reveal itself as a joke, a spoof of the fashion calendar I had been forced to follow. But no, this thing was in dead earnest. Fashion editor Jackie White had printed four pictures of me in various outfits crossing the street. "What should she have worn under the circumstances?" she asked. On day one I'd worn a navy blazer, for authority and credibility, of course. But what on earth had been in my mind when I changed to more relaxed, casual mood and wore short-sleeved blouses, cotton sweaters and skirts? How about the stifling temperatures and humidity, Jackie?

She asked John T. Molloy, author of "Dress for Success," what he would have done. He would have taken pictures of me in various outfits and shown them to people in a community similar to Kansas City, to see how they reacted. Said Mr. Molloy, "The outfit that evoked the response we wanted would be what she should wear."

Even the highly cosmetized mystery woman had something to say. It turned out that the overly attired female frequently at Replogle's arm had been none other than Cynthia Clark

Campbell, an assistant U.S. attorney in Kansas City. Her office was in the Federal building. Did she have an interest in the federal issues at question? She was quoted as saying, "I would have looked more professional. I would have worn a suit, business clothes." I had to admit, Miss Clark certainly looked like a pro.

The columnist interviewed a horde of "experts" and claimed that my lawyers had refused to discuss our "fashion strategy." She ended her article by citing the opinion of a law professor at the University of Missouri: "One (axiom) has always been to wear what you'd wear to church and you'd be safe."

That Sunday at Mass, I jokingly asked the young Jesuit outside St. Thomas More if God would allow me to attend Mass dressed as I was. He assured me with a wink that it would be all right, just this one time. It was my first awareness that God cares about what worshippers wear. I hoped He wouldn't mind my summery frock too much.

Dennis and Sarah had never said anything about my clothes. The long weekend ended. The jury finished their deliberations after about ten hours.

We were all called back into the courtroom. My pal, Pat Stockwell, a former assignment editor at Channel 9 living in California, had managed to race across the country in his jalopy and arrive just minutes before the verdict was read.

I could feel my heart beat as we strained to hear the verdicts.

On count one, or sex discrimination in advisory capacity, "We find in favor of Christine Craft."

On count two, Equal Pay Act, "We find in favor of Metromedia."

On count three, the Fraud, "We, in jury, find in favor of Christine Craft and assess the damages at $375,000."

Stockwell and I beamed at each other from across the courtroom. Dennis and Sarah and the rest of the team were filled with the joy of jury vindication.

The lawyers argued for ten minutes on the question of punitive damages. The jury quickly returned with an additional levy against Metromedia of $125,000.

We had won most of the first round, and I was thrilled. I was soon to be the half-million dollar headline baby. I had less than twelve dollars left to my name.

7.

THE GAG ORDER and the silence were both over. Outside, a milling mob of reporters waited for the chance to ask their questions and for the principals to make their statements.

But first, rising from the defense table, Donald Giffin did his equivalent of the tennis player jumping over the net after a losing match. "Your counsel did a very, very good job." I was slightly annoyed at the implications in his words: my case had not required my counsel to be miracle workers. I acknowledged that "Dennis and Sarah well represented the suit."

We could be much less terse outside to the assembled media. Operating on my reserve energy tanks, fueled by pure exhilaration, and forgetting all the cumulative fatigue, I had three basic convictions to relate. The jury's verdict had been a victory for civil rights, for women's rights, and for the rights of men and women television journalists who wanted their profession to have substantive integrity.

Yes, employers have the right to hire and fire as they see fit, but they don't have the right to flout the tenets of the Civil Rights act with impunity. They don't have the right to commit fraud—a civil crime. And no, I hadn't meant this trial to be an indictment of all television news. If it had become that, it was perhaps because Metromedia had claimed that their own questionable sexist practices were used industry-wide.

I would leave it to the pundits to ascertain what effects these verdicts would have on TV news in the future. The judge had still to make his own rulings on sex discrimination. The way the law was adjudicated, the jury's verdict was only "advisory." I had no doubt that Metromedia would ask the judge to throw out the fraud award, as well. We had certainly won a major battle, but it was far too soon to say we'd won the war.

For the moment, we were beset by requests for interviews. The reporters who had spent the most time in the courtroom were the ones with whom I chose to talk. After Howard Rosenberg, who hadn't missed a beat, there was Jeanne Wolfe of *Entertainment Tonight*. She had spent many hours on those unyielding courtroom benches, listening intently to convoluted testimony that helped make her daily stories more accurate than some of the half-baked efforts of the less attentive.

Cassandra Clayton of NBC News, in my estimation, had done rigorous background work for covering the case. We did an interview where Cassandra asked the question I didn't particularly want to answer: did I think I'd be blacklisted as a trouble-maker? Of course, we both knew the probable answer to that question. I still hoped I would not be blacklisted, but I was far less naive than many may have presumed.

The logic was simple. If I found myself blacklisted for speaking out against discrimination and fraud in an enterprise which is supposed to seek truth, maybe television news wasn't something I wanted to do anyway.

Of course, I theoretically still had the Santa Barbara job. But a nagging thought recurred that perhaps I would not be able to go home again, this time, so easily. The new news director at KEYT had left me with the quick impression that she represented everything I had just finished railing against. I wasn't sure; at that time it was just a premonition. The main thing I had seen this woman do so far in the Santa Barbara newsroom was make manicure appointments.

More pressing matters were still in Kansas City. First, there was the request from ABC's "Nightline" to be interrogated live late that evening. In addition, KMBC's new director had also sent a note asking me to take part in a special half-hour program immediately following the "Nightline" broadcast. When could they pre-tape the interview? Channel 9 had asked. "Tape?" I had answered. "I will be glad to do this interview, but only if it is live, not taped." Sputter, choke, gasp. "Oh well, yes, of course, live absolutely."

I made time to place some calls home. "Hi Mom, Hi Dad, yes I know you are ecstatic. Dad, I was wondering if you could help me out with my September rent?" Dad said he would, figuring that his daughter wasn't such a bad risk, the alleged half-millionairess. My mother assured me that they were geared up to watch the network newscasts and that they'd stay up for "Nightline," even though it was past their bedtime.

Bob Hamilton was equally jubilant and had his videocassette recorder in the ready mode.

I gave King Harris of KEYT all he needed for the Santa Barbara newscast and warned him not to get too cozy with the substitute co-anchorette. I'd soon be home to give him the bad time he was so used to. "Oh, by the way," he told me, "You've got stacks of mail and phone messages, and I'm very, very proud of you."

Somewhere in the midst of all the high-flying confusion, a reporter asked if it were true that I had already signed a movie deal for a five-figure sum.

In fact, more than a year before, Susan Williams, a novice producer from Los Angeles, had approached me about optioning the rights to the story.

Susan came to rallies and fund-raisers, expressing a genuine understanding. I eventually signed an agreement to allow her to develop the idea. I had not received any money (just gas fare to Beverly Hills and some linguine with clam sauce) nor would I until an actual movie was made. If that were to happen, I would be paid five figures, $25,000, plus points.

I figured that a television movie or a feature done well would only create more dialogue and focus more consciousness on sexual inequality and the companion themes.

Bob Hamilton was upset that I hadn't consulted him about making the agreement. But I had to trust my instincts. If I had premeditated making a lucrative movie deal, I could have pursued Bob's connections, but I chose not to. I certainly did not want to give Metromedia any chance to point to Bob profiting from my situation.

Entertainment Tonight's Catherine Mann asked me if I wanted to play myself. "No," I told her, but I'd be a technical advisor. "You know what they do. They sit on the set in a chair with their name stenciled across the back. They are tied to the chairs and have a gag and a blindfold both firmly in place."

As for the casting we both laughed. "Try Dyan Cannon (too old, too pretty) or that spunky Sharon Gless (right age, too pretty), or Barbie Benton with wrinkles (too deferential), I don't care who they get, just so long as she does a great job."

After all, since nearly every cab driver in Hollywood carries a script on the front seat, the chances of a movie ever being made were miniscule.

Having explained all that to the Kansas City reporter, I had only time enough to eat some fast food chicken wings and apply a daub of lipgloss. Soon I found myself wired to an earpiece, sitting in front of a network camera, hopefully ready for Sam Donaldson's questions on "Nightline."

Since Donaldson was the foremost protagonist of quality journalism on the White House beat, a sort of Peck's bad boy, I knew he'd ask tough questions.

ABC had invited Metromedia to take part in the broadcast, but they had refused. To provide some sort of strange balance on the program, ABC scrounged up one of the few over-forty female anchors in the country and one of the rare female news directors.

Anne Bishop of WPLG in Florida denied that her aging looks were ever a problem and referred to news as a "product" that must be packaged to garner the largest possible audience. News director, Kristin Ostrowski of WEWS in Cleveland, expressed her fear that the verdict would in some way hinder management in its hiring and firing.

I made the point that my case was specific. I hoped there

would be more aging on-air females like Anne Bishop. I hoped other news directors would not be able to treat people fraudulently or violate the tenets of the Civil Rights Act.

I asked Sam a question to illustrate the most germane point. Hypothetically, if ABC had decided to remove him from his correspondency because he didn't hide his intelligence to make women White House correspondents look smarter, wouldn't his feathers be ruffled? Wouldn't he possibly even make a federal case out of it?

There was just the famed impish Donaldson semi-smile in response to that one. But, he continued, what about the surveys that I had fared poorly in? I reminded him that he should know better than most that you can't please all the people all the time. Our jobs are not to please but to bring the news, raise the provocative issues of the day, not to titillate or make the viewer comfy. In addition, research can be used as a tool for making management decisions, but it should be research without predetermined bias, and based on defensible criteria.

"Nightline" also asked Howard Rosenberg for his critic's comments. He was unabashed in his satisfaction that I had at least won two-thirds of the issues. He did say it was too soon to judge the full impact, but he believed I had become a role model for other women TV journalists who would like to continue their professions without discrimination. He also declared that the trial process, at the very least, had provided an illuminating primer on the practices of TV news. The sancrosanct promotional armor of at least one television station had been seen to be full of rusting chinks. If the public depended on local news for its information, then the public deserved to demand the best.

As "Nightline" wrapped up, Channel 9 finished preparations for its own half-hour live special. Anchor Larry Moore introduced the program, showed some background footage on the events of the past two weeks and then went live to me. I answered his rather unoriginal questions, politely, but not deferentially. Then I had a question for Larry Moore, or rather for the management of Channel 9.

They had promoted the concept to the Kansas City public that every night during the trial at 10 P.M. they would have a sex discrimination trial lawyer on their newscast to give her expert opinion on the legal issues at hand. I asked Larry why they had chosen to use someone who rarely spent more than a half-hour in the courtroom, who was not a Title VII lawyer, and who just happened to be blond, young and telegenic? Moore lost his usual programmed composure, mumbled an unheard reply, and quickly went to commercial. I was not seen on the rest of that program. Instead, they came back after the break with the attorney in question. He asked her about my charges and she replied in a fidgity fashion. All right, so she hadn't heard all the testimony, but she'd been "briefed by the experts at Channel 9" every night before going on the air. A supposedly neutral observer had been briefed solely by the defendant as to the important issues of the trial! It was the illusion of credibility at its finest. I'm sure that many late night viewers saw the transparency of Channel 9's hype. The station may have been owned by a different corporation, but R. Kent Replogle was still in charge. His practices clearly had the Hearst corporation's imprimatur, as well as Metromedia's.

Well after midnight, Howard Rosenberg gave me a lift back to Marty's house. There over milk and cookies we did a very candid and casual interview. "It's not over till it's over, Howard. After those verdicts, I felt like doing a triple jump. But the strongest instinct I have right now is one of caution. I think it's going to be a bit of a boxing match. Don't you agree? Or am I being paranoid and overly negative?"

"Probably just a bit too negative," he said soothingly. He encouraged me to enjoy the day's victory while it was sweet. Who knew how long it would take before the whole thing was over? At that very moment I looked like I hadn't slept in forty-eight hours. I had to be up by four A.M. to face the battle of the network limousines.

That morning the alarm rang at three. I rousted myself, got ready, looked out the window to see the NBC limo waiting just outside, idling in the pitch black. When I got to the car, there was Cassandra, orange juice and giant coffee mug in hand, ready to whisk me off to WDAF and their satellite downlink. "Wake up, Christine, it's time for you to meet Jane Pauley."

Even though I couldn't see her and even though there was an audio delay that made it very difficult to be conversational, I could tell by the tone of Jane's voice that she was tickled pink by my winning. Press accounts later that day quoted her as saying she'd been "surprised but pleased by the legal victory. Christine Craft also won a moral victory because her case was so persuasive."

As I emerged from WDAF, the CBS limo complete with producer and donuts was on hand to whisk me at breakneck speed to KCMO. The CBS station was providing the facilities for another interview, this one with Diane Sawyer.

"Did I think my award would really mean any changes in TV news?" I answered as truthfully as I could. "I have no illusions that this is going to make a huge difference in TV news. But if it keeps one news director at one station, someplace, sometime from doing the same thing, I hope it does that."

After the whirl of the morning shows and a round of heartfelt goodbyes to Kansas City friends, I headed back to Santa Barbara. The flight attendants were sweet, sneaking me into the virtually empty first class section of the plane. They told me their stories of sex and age discrimination in the airline industry. Despite landmark rulings barring unequal treatment, the deeply ingrained remnants of old sexist and ageist patterns die hard. My victory had been a reminder to them that someone always has to speak out, just to keep the machinery of fair treatment from slipping into reverse.

Three seats and two aisles to the right, a voice emerged, "Hey, doll, can I have another Jack Daniels rocks?"

An Anchorwoman's Story 155

WITH A BOUQUET of native flowers Bob met me at the tiny Santa Barbara airport. There was also a camera crew from Los Angeles, complete with Stanley Seigal, peripatetic interviewer of celebrities, instant and otherwise.

In a t-shirt and sweats, clutching my bouquet, I withstood the barrage of questions from this unexpected interviewer. I couldn't wait to get home to the solitude of the empty beach. My legs near atrophied from the courtroom's frozen postures, I longed to let Brinkley lead me on a full-bore sprint atop the wet, hard sand.

Soon enough I was yelling to him not to roll on the dead seal. In blatant disregard of that order, he took a dive and came up dog-smiling at me, as if I'd never been gone. I knew once again, as I've known since childhood, that the twin magic of the ocean and the shore is my constant source of regenerative energy. I return to it always with reverence. It never disappoints. If I go too long without seeing and touching and smelling it, a vital part of my soul begins to wither.

Back home one week before my month's leave of absence was over, I was anxious to return to work ahead of schedule. I quickly found that the new news director was not at all eager for me to return. Why, she had already done the schedule for the upcoming week and she didn't feel like changing it. The young woman who had replaced me called to congratulate me and tell me she hated anchoring and couldn't understand why the news director was trying to establish an unwarranted rivalry between us. Fresh out of law school, she had taken her first real job as a reporter. Patti Paniccia had never even wanted to anchor. She dreamed of being a legal reporter, not an anchor. At any rate, she felt uncomfortable and out of place being asked to do something where she had no experience.

Patti and I were to become good friends, sharing as we did some striking similarities. Both of us had been competitive surfers, though in different eras. This was simply not a case of the younger, prettier woman wanting to take over the more visible job. Like me, Patti Paniccia was an independent spirit. She was not easily molded into the type of jealous, scheming TV "climber" that perhaps her boss had expected.

Station owner Bill Luton, Sr., called to apologize. He had heard, after the fact, what the new management employee had done. He also gave me his personal expression of congratulation. I didn't feel that the Lutons had told this woman to ease me out. I knew, however, that she seemed to have an extreme dislike for both me and King Harris. Perhaps she just resented the people who technically knew how to produce the newscast, people she hadn't chosen, people with no intrinsic debt to her. She had bragged of her experience as a reporter for television station KNXT in Los Angeles. Contacts in Los Angeles confirmed what we all perceived: she had never been a television reporter.

I used my extra week of time to do a little extraneous television. I was honored to be asked to appear on two of my favorite programs, "Donahue" and "Late Night with David Letterman."

In Chicago on the "Donahue" segment, there were two other guests, a TV image consultant and veteran NBC consumer reporter, Betty Furness. Betty had been fighting my type of battle successfully for many years. At sixty-seven she was in that tiny percentile of "older" women still prominent on the air. She was cautious when we were first introduced. Clearly it would be counterproductive to rally to the cause of someone she had never met. By the time we'd had a chance to talk and the tape was rolling, Betty was intelligently effusive in her praise of my efforts. She remarked that I was pretty, but not too pretty to be distracting. She chronicled her own history, starting with evening gowns and Westinghouse refrigerators, to her well-known niche on the "Today Show" and her active reporting for the New York NBC affiliate. She acknowledged that too few women had been allowed by the men in charge to stay on the air after they started showing signs of feminine aging. I hoped she knew what a fantastic boost she had given my spirits. She hinted merrily that she'd recommend me to those she knew for future employment as a TV journalist. Though we both sensed that my continuing job prospects in television news were certainly dubious, it was a darling and upbeat thing for her to say.

Actually, just being around the ever tousleable Phil Donahue is enough to give anyone a booster shot of effusive energy. I adore his style when he's on a roll. There he prods and counterpunches and provokes those all-embracing dialogues on the questions of fairness in American affairs.

During our encounter, he mock-assaulted me with the contention that people really watch the news because they are charmed by this or that newscaster. "Phil, journalists should not have to worry about winning personality contests," I replied. He looked at me and twinkling with full intensity blasted, "Yes, but America rewards kissing babies!" I fired back, "And other things."

I was getting a reputation for outspokenness.

In New York the next day I was grilled on WNBC's "Live at Five" by none other than Sue Simmons, the woman Lynn Wilford had told me was "too assertive." She turned out to be assertive, asking the meanest-edged questions anyone had so far. She quoted a *New York* magazine item that I had upset Kansas Citians by bragging about California. I could only reply that I hadn't. I mentioned the fact of the upwardly mobile ratings and questioned the credibility of *New York* magazine establishing itself as an arbiter of taste in Kansas City.

It was a tough interview. But Betty Furness was in the wings acting, as she described herself, as my fairy godmother. She introduced me to the other members of the WNBC talent stable. She had been there since the earliest days of network television and was quite a guide. After a while, Betty ushered me across the hall to the Letterman studio and wished me a safe journey home.

Suddenly I was a bundle of nerves. This was the show I

stayed up late to watch every night along with NBC's terrific news overview, "Overnight."

No one could induce side-splitting laughter like David Letterman. Sometimes I'd wake up my dogs to watch "stupid pet tricks," a regular feature on the program. They'd wag their tails, as I'd pound on my wall, contorted in an uncontrollable spasm of glee as some poor Pomeranian balanced a milk bone on his snout.

Not only is Letterman terminally funny; he is to me and millions terminally cute. Bandleader Paul Schafer cooled my jitters by telling me I looked quite glamorous. Nonetheless, after the first part of the interview, I leaned over to tell Letterman that I was just a bit intimidated by it all. He pooh poohed that in his own very high-strung fashion. I realized that he was probably perpetually more nervous than I was. After that I relaxed, had a great time joking about my supposed "muttness" and the idiocies of TV consultantism. Dog lover that he is, David most enjoyed the third segment of the interview when we discussed the surfing ability of my trusty Brinkley. Letterman had given me a chance to be something other than a crusading activist.

Leaving New York on an upnote, I spent some time with a man who made an interesting proposal; Carleton Sedgeley was one of a number of lecture agents who approached me with the idea of giving speeches all over the country for healthy fees. He and his wife, Lucy, and their staff had a small but prestigious group of lecturers. They exclusively represented Dick Cavett, Vincent Price, Nora Ephron and Carl Bernstein (separately not together), Edwin Moses, Betty Williams and an impressive list of others.

Carleton was realistic in describing what he felt lecturing could mean for me. He felt I had conducted myself well in the post-trial interviews, that I would probably have little trouble addressing large audiences, that I was an anchorwoman who could work without the safety net of the teleprompter. I was a hot commodity at the moment. That public curiosity could be turned to my own advantage if I were willing to take certain risks. Going on the lecture circuit is like taking the brass ring on the merry-go-round. You either go for it or you don't. If you do decide to seize the moment, there is no guarantee how long you will stay a marketable lecture commodity.

Although it would be very tenuous, lecturing would certainly help my financial situation even if I just managed to do it on weekends. I still owed the law firm $16,000 for out-of-pocket expenses. Seeing any of the money I had won from that first jury was far from being a reality. I told Carleton Sedgeley that I'd consider his offer carefully. He told me he could arrange weekend lectures if I chose to stay at KEYT. But he also emphasized that to take good advantage of the current interest in my case, he would prefer to book me on a full-time tour. He outlined his agency fees of 35 percent and calculated what a reasonable income for a six month period could be. I was certainly intrigued, and I liked his candor, but in no way was I sure that I'd take his offer. Everything was in flux.

Back on the job for just four days in Santa Barbara, I found my concentration sadly lacking. Every time the AP wire would ring, I'd jump up to see if Judge Stevens had issued his rulings in *my* case. As I had expected, Metromedia had immediately asked Judge Stevens to throw out everything we had won. I was needfully self-absorbed and not giving full attention to the work at hand.

Then, at the end of that fourth day, a demoralizing situation helped me decide about the immediate future. One of the local Santa Barbara city councilwomen was announcing her candidacy for a second term. A rather shy lady with no major political ambitions beyond her current job, Jeanne Graffy had been a little intimidated when surrounded by cameras and tape recorders and reporters as she announced on the steps of city hall.

King and I had noticed that the story was in the first block of the newscast, but we hadn't had a chance to listen to the actual soundbite from Ms. Graffy. On the air, King read the into to the story: "Jeanne Graffy announced for a second term today, but in the middle of her remarks, she seemed to get lost." As we looked at each other questioning the strange copy, there followed seventeen seconds of Jeanne Graffy painfully stumbling and fumbling for words. Then there was another cut of her describing her attitude about downtown development. We both wondered what the hell the purpose had been in humiliating Jeanne Graffy. The news director was gone for the day, and we asked the reporter who had covered the announcement. He told us that Ms. Graffy had lost her place in her remarks, laughed and had said, "I'm sorry, can we start over?" All the reporters there had said, "Sure Jeanne, do it again." She had. It was no big deal. There was nothing unexpected in her renewed candidacy. Furthermore, one's own good word has usually been enough in Santa Barbara. Apparently it hadn't been for KEYT's news director. When the reporter casually mentioned that the councilwoman had flubbed and lost her place, the executive news directress barked "Lead with it!" The public had the right to know what kind of person they were being asked to vote for.

That night at eleven, as King and I always produced the late newscast, we deleted the fumbling portion and merely used the statement of Graffy's reasons for running again. The next morning, the boss phoned King and read him the riot act. He was never, never, never to change anything, anything at all in a newscast without her approval. Of course, she would not be there at night to supervise production of the news in a town she knew nothing about. Therefore, all we could do for the late news, given this command and our limited resources, was rerun the earlier newscast. She was determined to let us know who had the power. She would use it without regard to humanity or common sense.

Had I been less distracted, I would have stuck it out, waiting for this woman to be fired as she eventually was. But I knew my current temperament would not allow me to be diplomatic with such a mean-spirited person. I did have some options. I sent a telegram: "Profoundly disturbed by your news decisions affecting our community, I resign effective immediately. Letters to follow to the Lutons." In my letters, I described my own observations of this news room "leader," who regaled female employees with descriptions of her multiple orgasms and where to find the best false fingernails. I explained that though I loved KEYT, I could not pledge fealty to someone I found so lacking in essential ability. I also told them that the combination of factors made it impossible for me to give one hundred percent to my job at the moment. I told them I wanted to take the opportunity at hand.

The decision to leave was the hardest of all to make. I knew I'd be opening myself up for criticism. In one fell swoop I would no longer be the martyred mutt, I'd be the "opportunist mutt." I signed a contract with Carleton Sedgeley for a collegiate tour.

Bill Luton, Sr., called to express his disappointment at my impulsive gesture. But from his heart he wished me godspeed.

I had agreed to do a couple of free lectures prior to beginning with the agency. The first took me to Wichita to address the local Kansas reporters at the Wichita Ramada.

When I returned home, I walked in the door to find my house sitters cracking up from a joke Joan Rivers had just made on some awards show. They told me I probably wouldn't like it. "Christine Craft won half a million dollars and spent half of it on cosmetics." I was supposed to be flattered at having been chosen for target practice.

Then there were the scores of commentaries usually with the same theme as that of Barbara Holsopple in the *Pittsburgh Press*. "CHRISTINE CRAFT'S TV VICTORY IS LUCRATIVE, BUT SHALLOW." I had the urge to write and tell her that she had it all wrong. Deeply in debt, I knew it hadn't been lucrative, but I was hearing from women in every city that I travelled to that it had affected their lives. That was not shallow, but profoundly meaningful.

Anchor Pat Miles of Minneapolis-St. Paul said, "I think it's going to have implications for women in broadcasting that *ultimately* will be very good. The substance of the job is going to be placed above cosmetics."

In Los Angeles, anchor Christine Lund of KABC was quoted, "This judgment will serve as a large broom to the backside of management, especially in small and medium markets. Management will have to reassess how they treat women. Research is a disastrous idea. It runs counter to what the news dissemination business is all about. It is a source of embarrassment to every co-worker." She added that she felt the trial's outcome might prevent the need for further similar lawsuits. "No management wants to undergo public scrutiny and be publicly embarrassed."

Reuben Frank, president of NBC News, said, "I think what will happen is that the legal departments will instruct news executives on what to say. They will have little seminars all over the country. That will be the chief result." I had to agree that would be *one* of the chief results.

I got a real kick out of Judy Mann in the *Washington Post:*

> While this is important to women in communications, it is also important in a broader sense for the American public. Television, whatever else it does, is a mirror of society.
>
> The Craft case shows that the mirror does not come close to reflecting the presence and interests of half of society. It is as distorted a picture of America as an amusement hall mirror.
>
> The finding in Craft's case should make it easier for current newswomen, most of whom are now in their late 30s, to grow older on the air, just as say Dan Rather, 51, has done.
>
> Beyond that, Craft at considerable risk of personal embarrassment, has drawn unprecedented attention to the fact that television is still a man's world, with ugly double standards. Her victory serves notice on broad-

casters that the drive by women for equal employment opportunities in the industry is far from over.

And with $500,000 judgments, the industry may discover just how costly cosmetics can be.

Armed with my experience and all the input from others, I set out to colleges and universities, and state bar associations and women's groups all over the country. I spoke extemporaneously, giving basically the narrative account. I spent time with students both before and after lectures, generally expanding my own consciousness of the country and every region of it. Everywhere I went, from Canada to the deep South, there were volatile question-and-answer sessions after every lecture. Though many of the questions were understandably the same, the interest was genuine enough to keep me inspired though road-weary.

One day I read a column by William F. Buckley, Jr. Widely syndicated, it was entitled "Potty little court." It urged Judge Stevens, who you may remember was short of stature, to overturn the advisory sex discrimination verdict in my favor and to disallow the monetary award granted on the fraud count. Buckley argued: "In Kansas City, the management established that Miss Craft was not fetching the audience that management thought it ought to have. Now, one should instantly recognize that that failure in Miss Craft by no means says about her anything at all disagreeable. Some of our best friends are lousy on television, and we do not doubt that Socrates could never have made it as an anchorman, even on PBS."

Surely I had often thought how kind it was of PBS to allow Mr. Buckley's twitching forehead and sphincter-like mouth such abundant air time. But regardless of his looks, Mr. Buckley had his facts wrong this time. Ratings and revenues had risen during my tenure. That had been amply demonstrated in court.

His sophistic remarks continued with a warning for the

court and other Buckley ideologues: "Check with a judge before you promote or demote, because otherwise you may run into one of those civil rights statutes that are being interpreted as permanently protecting women, blacks, homosexuals—who knows where the list will end—from the normal vicissitudes of democratic life."

"Up your *vicissitudes,* Mr. Buckley," I thought as I read his bigoted analysis. But William Buckley was probably feeling no pain at all when Joseph Stevens handed down his rulings soon after, on Halloween of that same year.

Stevens rejected the jury on sex discrimination, strangely citing that not only had I not been discriminated against but that: "Her affinity for the casual beach life and her apparent indifference to matters of appearance required defendant to formulate and implement corrective measures appropriate to her unique circumstances."

Corrective measures? I hadn't noticed that there were any beaches in Kansas City.

He upheld Metromedia on the equal pay act claim in three brief sentences.

He threw out my award and ordered a retrial on the fraud issue, to be tried at "9:30 A.M. on Wednesday, January 4, 1984, at the Federal Courthouse in Joplin, Missouri; a jury of twelve will be impaneled and will be sequestered throughout the proceedings."

He justified the new trial—the time and unbelievable expense (to plaintiff)—on the grounds that in the first trial, "the jury became so infected with passion and prejudice that it was unable to discharge its duty of fairness to both parties." He was decrying the fact that the first jury had not been sequestered and that it had not come to the decisions he would have preferred.

He declared openly his opinion that I had never been told I was "too old, too unattractive, and not sufficiently deferential to men." This was in spite of Scott's collaborating testimony. I was reeling, but not yet on the ropes.

That was before I learned he had declared himself judge for the second trial. What unmitigated gall, the potty little court!

When Dennis and Sarah reached me with word of Judge Stevens's Halloween treat, I happened to be in Milwaukee to address both the Milwaukee Press Club and the Society of Professional Journalists. Depressed as the three of us were, we certainly weren't ready to throw in the towel yet. They sent me a message of support and continuing commitment from Kansas City. I would have to face the music of "failure" in front of the Milwaukee audience of reporters there to attend the banquet and speech.

There was no place to hide. A crew from ABC's "Nightline" set up in a room down from the banquet hall. Correspondent Lynn Scherr, who was hosting that program, would take a late night look at me, up close and personal. Was I down? Was I out? Did I still dare to think I could win it?

By the next day, I still hadn't cried "Uncle." On the CBS Morning News, Diane Sawyer cited the judge's ruling and asked me via satellite if I really was "unique among women" in my lack of appearance skills.

I replied that I had always been well-scrubbed and that I had every intention of winning in Joplin.

The fact that our first triumph so far had been ideological rather than monetary only strengthened my resolve and my patience. I determined that I would also no longer resist addressing the more obvious political implications of this legal battle.

A presidential election would be occurring nine months after our date in Joplin. My experience had taught me that the "trickle-down" theory of civil rights was definitely not good enough for a nation which preached justice for all. The Reagan Administration frequently argued that American women did not need an Equal Rights Amendment. Existing law was supposed to be sufficient to seek redress for the "problems" of sex discrimination. My case was nothing less than a test of that theory. Clearly, even if one could raise the money to seek redress, the system was faulty. Jury verdicts meant nothing in sex discrimination cases. If you happened to draw a sexist judge, as we had, you had no chance at all of achieving a fair result. The judge could just dismiss all the jury's hard work.

Syndicated columnist Joseph Kraft in the *Washington Post* had written of the current political climate vis-à-vis women's rights. In a column dubbed "Women's Rights and Wrongs," he cited an incident from the long hot summer of 1983. At the international convention of the Federation of Business and Professional Women, Reagan had declared he "recognized women's place," because he said, "I happen to be one who believes that if it wasn't for women, us men would be walking around in skin suits carrying clubs."

The BPW women were appalled at Reagan's condescending remarks. They found nothing honorable or equitable about having themselves defined as mere accoutrements to male progress.

Kraft wrote, "the fact is that sex discrimination is widely practiced in many fields, including broadcasting. Many women of high intelligence find their abilities underrated because they are not what men call 'attractive.' For those women and their cause, the finding of the Kansas City jury was a notable boost."

He concluded, "Despite recent gains, or maybe even because of them, many women remain dissatisfied with their lot in American life. They complain, and they even sue, because they feel they have strong reason for discontent."

"No wise person, least of all in political life, will trifle with those feelings. That Reagan would try to laugh them off is only one more sign of how out of touch he is with the serious elements of national life."

THE LECTURE TOUR provided a provocative forum for expressing and debating those ideas. I would not hesitate to point out the obvious sexist bias of the Reagan-appointed

...AND SO THE CRAFT CASE HAS DEFINITELY CHANGED THE COURSE OF TV NEWS, THINGS WILL NEVER BE THE SAME... NOW BACK TO MY PRETTY, YOUNG, DEFERRING, UNDERPAID CO-ANCHOR...
KANSAS CITY STAR
NEWS

judge with whom we had been and would continue to be saddled.

Dennis, Sarah and I had wanted to ask the Eighth Circuit Court to remove Stevens from presiding over the second trial. Didn't we at least deserve a jurist who hadn't already formed an opinion? Didn't we deserve at least to have the admission of evidence determined by someone who would base decisions on the law and the evidence and not on his own prejudice? Of course we did, but other politics intervened. The law firm to which I owned considerable out-of-pocket monies had other cases coming up in front of Stevens. They didn't want Stevens to be embarrassed by being removed for bias by a higher court. I had no clout to pressure the firm's major partners to support us in having Stevens disqualified. I didn't have the funds to force the firm into doing the ethical thing and so we were stuck with our kangaroo court.

So much for the hierarchy. After a few more lectures talking to people at a different level, I found myself better motivated to face the seemingly stacked deck of Joplin, Mo. After all, the bottom line was that if six people in Kansas City could perceive who was telling the truth and who was not, then twelve people in Joplin, Missouri, could also.

If a motel maid in North Carolina could slip me two dollars and tell me not to give up, adding "You are fighting for all of us," I ought to be able to persist.

Metromedia, by their refusal to admit they were wrong after the jury's verdict, was creating the very *cause célèbre* they had accused me of inventing through Bob Hamilton. My sense of outrage was heightened by the fact that the case had been deliberately moved to a small conservative community where we would only be allowed to try a third of our case, perhaps even less than that. But Dennis and Sarah and I were determined to see this battle through to a fair conclusion.

8.

METROMEDIA MUST HAVE figured that they would have a tough time winning their case in front of a jury, even with all the advantages that had been thrown their way. So their next tack was to try to intimidate me by digging up some dirt. They must have thought they had struck gold when they hired for their station in Houston a brand new female co-anchor who promptly told a Houston *Chronicle* TV editor the following tale.

Ginger Casey had worked briefly as a co-anchor at KEYT in Santa Barbara during part of the time I had been in Kansas City. She told Ann Hodges of the *Chronicle* that she had been fired so that KEYT could hire me back.

Ginger Casey went on to disclose to the reporter that she had been told that KEYT didn't like her looks and that was why they were firing her. Casey also claimed that I had been fired earlier from Santa Barbara, had sued KEYT, and had won. According to Casey, Craft had been hired as an anchor/reporter, and "when they didn't like her work as an anchor, they took her off and made her a camera person. She sued because she said she had been hired as an anchor, and she won. She got $8,000 in damages, and that's when she went to Kansas City. She does have a reputation for suing people."

Casey, remembered in Santa Barbara for her habit of wearing a large gold-plated gingerbread man pin on her lapel while anchoring at KEYT, added, "She's very nice, but maybe she just wasn't good."

I wondered how on earth Ginger Casey could know if I was "very nice" or "not very good," since I didn't think we had ever met. Considering who had just employed her, I wasn't surprised, on the one hand; but on the other, I was amazed that her information was so terribly botched.

She had also told her new Metromedia news director that I had been an extremely difficult person to work with and that I had been fired from several other stations.

The national media jumped on this story, questioning why, if I had been so difficult to work with, I had been hired back at the same station that I had supposedly sued.

They asked KEYT management for a comment. Bill Luton, Jr., told them that Casey's departure from KEYT was in no way related to my return. He questioned her motivation in making the remarks. "If you don't want to draw attention to yourself, don't wave your arms." He also remarked that Casey's comments were mistaken in their references to an alleged lawsuit. KEYT, he said, had never had a troublesome relationship with me and they would never have rehired me if they had. "We're happy to have her back, as we were the first time she came back," he added.

Ms. Casey replied to Luton's response that she was "mortified and embarrassed" by the publicity her comments had received. She had just been "sharing lunch with a reporter." Perhaps she had now learned one of those basic tenets of the rough-and-tumble world of journalism. Unless otherwise agreed upon, when you gossip to another reporter, it's not off-the-record, even if it's over the most civilized of lunches.

Radio and TV commentator Paul Harvey blew the story beyond its already absurd proportions by claiming I had beaten KEYT out of $800,000.

I had never sued KEYT, or even considered such a thing. But there had been undercurrents of tension in that newsroom. For example: When Ronald Reagan had just won the votes to assure the Republican nomination in 1980, he gave his news conference at our station, which was in close proximity to his ranch.

That particular day, I had made the mistake of wearing

pants to work. I guess I just hadn't remembered that when Nancy Reagan was first lady of my state, she had tried to issue an edict that the women in state government had to wear skirts. Someone had reminded her at the time that she didn't have that authority.

That night, other reporters had been assigned to interview Ron and Nancy. I had been on my dinner hour when they arrived. Coming through the back door, as was my habit, I noticed all the hubbub in the studio where the interviews were being conducted. On tippietoes I walked as quietly as I could across the cement floor, listened attentively to a few of the questions and answers, then went quietly out to do the work of producing our eleven o'clock newscast, less than two hours away.

A few days later, the news director (to remain unnamed) called me in and said that it had been brought to the attention of higher management that I was "not expressing pro-Reagan sentiment," whoops, he meant I *was* expressing "anti-Reagan sentiment," and that I shouldn't do that. I asked him what he was referring to, adding that I hadn't been expressing pro or anti-anyone sentiments. Did he have an air-check to demonstrate what he meant? No, he didn't, but I should be careful. In the meantime, I was being taken off the late-night anchor duty, reassigned to anchor the early news sportscast and continue reporting. I said nothing other than that I would agree to those changes.

A week later, he called me into his office along with my co-anchor, telling us that we'd both been terminated because we had failed to be flexible. We also had not shot enough film stories lately, as our union contract said we could be required to do.

My co-anchor, Phil, had never been asked to shoot *anything*, and I had always been more than willing to shoot because I enjoyed it so much.

There had always been rancor between this boss and Phil. Phil, with his blond organized manner and dislike of social drinking, had not curried much favor with his boozy and swarthy superior.

Phil and I asked our Union (NABET) if we could get some help with this problem. They were extremely supportive and presented the information to highest management, which had been unaware of the specifics.

Mr. Luton Senior asked me to lunch to tell him my side of what had happened. A staunch supporter and friend of President Reagan, he nonetheless knew that whatever my political views, I had not been unprofessional on the air.

The disagreement was quickly settled and Phil and I were soon back to work. There was no publicity about the incident, which had occurred many months before KMBC had first approached me. KEYT's owners had been fair, as always. Persistence in that matter had yielded success and even had helped me later stand up to Metromedia.

Ginger Casey, uninformed and hyperbolic, had made a big blunder. Metromedia assumed that there was a mountain just under her molehill and so they subpoenaed a long list of KEYT employees to take depositions for the second trial.

Perhaps they felt that I would drop my lawsuit because I didn't want to put my friends, colleagues, and former employers through the bother. Maybe, they thought, I'd quit because I had a deep dark secret that those depositions would reveal.

Well, it was *obnoxious* having to ask people to go through the deposition process. At least, I hope it was interesting for them. No dirty secrets were to be found. I sat in on every session I could, calculating silently the added expense that this little exercise in futility tacked onto my bills.

Witness after witness confirmed the truth of the incident; the only point Metromedia extracted was that at one time I had experienced a less than rosy situation at KEYT, and had weathered it well.

I was proud that KEYT had welcomed me back with open arms, not only once but twice.

Dennis's flights to Santa Barbara and numerous deposition fees were added to my out-of-pocket expenses.

Before I had too much time to dwell on that, Sarah and Dennis and I were packed into her compact car with our garment bags and extra toothbrushes leaving a Kansas City driveway. It was a clear bright January day with fields of whitest crystalline snowbanks lining the highway. What a way to start 1984! The road to Joplin stretched ahead.

There we could try only a third of our case, the fraud portion. Even that would likely be limited by the rulings of a hostile judge. It was nigh unto impossible to separate the sex discrimination from the fraud or any single charge from the others. We had been hog-tied, hamstrung, and half blindfolded.

On the vital admissibilty of evidence, Judge Stevens's first pronouncements pre-trial disallowed us from playing the focus group tapes. "They go to the fraud," Stevens agreed, "but they are too inflammatory." He wouldn't let them in.

The tapes actually offered key fraud evidence. If I had known when I went there that my tenure would be evaluated on my bleepability as compared with Anne Peterson or anyone else, I would not have gone! They had every right to know that, but the Joplin jury would hear only a selected portion of the fraud case. Of course the tapes were inflammatory, why the hell was I suing?

The jury themselves were chosen through an elaborate process which included questionnaires, lengthy *voir dire* sessions, and Judge Stevens's favorite question when determining if a prospective juror would be a fair one: "If you were either Metromedia or Christine Craft, would you feel comfortable with you as a juror?" Terrific question, but the way he usually analyzed their answers was, to say the least, troubling.

One prospective juror had said in the questionnaire that he thought the first trial had resulted in my being "unsatisfied" with a big settlement. Dennis asked him the tried and true question: "And if you were Christine Craft, would you want to have yourself sit as a juror in this case?" The man answered, "Perhaps." When Dennis pressed him whether he could be fair and impartial, he responded with a reluctant, "I think so." Dennis replied, "I need to know." Judge Stevens chimed in at this point with "I think we are really getting repetitious. Let's move on."

After the man had left, Giffin puffed up like a pigeon, offered that he thought the man was candid and reflective and would make an excellent juror. Dennis questioned his lack of impartiality. But Stevens overruled Dennis's challenge. This juror would be seated.

When another prospective venireman expressed the view that it was his gut feeling that my lawsuit was exorbitant, Judge Stevens found the man well-informed and thoughtful and overruled our first strike. Fortunately, as the process drew to a close, we were able to eliminate the earlier juror whom we had found objectionable. Eventually we ended up with a panel of six women and six men and two alternates. They were to be sequestered in a downtown hotel, shuffled in and out of Marshals' vans as they left each day for the courthouse, their every footfall through the wet snow recorded by the local news stations.

The principals were all staying at the Holiday Inn in Joplin: My team, their team, my witnesses, their witnesses, judge, clerk, court reporter and several journalists covering the second round. The weather stayed cold, damp and snowy, a clime when people go outside only when they have to. We all ate breakfast every morning in the same dining room, the air thick with anticipation not best for digestion. Seeing Ridge Shannon's wife in the laundry room, I'd wait until later to do mine. Accommodations were good, room service excellent, the satellite dish TV a late-night godsend.

The people of Joplin were downright friendly to us, honking their horns and flashing the victory sign when they'd see us crossing the street bundled up against the cold on the way to lunch. Dennis and I were given free two-week memberships to the YMCA. Every night after the sessions in court, Dennis could play handball and I could get in my half-hour of laps in a wonderful old white-tile pool that was just slightly over-chlorinated.

Waitresses would give me big mugs of coffee and hugs, murmuring, "We're pulling for you, Christine, don't let the bastards get you down!"

But the many rulings Judge Stevens made early on seemed determined to keep us down. I would not be allowed to testify to what Ridge Shannon had said to me the day I'd been removed as an anchor. Judge Stevens didn't like the expression, "too old, too unattractive, not deferential to men." It had been repeated "ad nauseum," he said. He wouldn't allow it in this trial. He wanted to limit our evidence only to those things that related to the few days in November where I had first been approached for the job.

I began to feel numb, the climate both inside and outside the courtroom was chilling. I sought a way to hibernate through this second rape of my psyche. Somehow I had to disconnect my emotions from flying off in an easy rage at the way we were being judicially screwed. We had to get the facts before this jury.

I noticed that now both the judge and Giffin would cringe concurrently every time I used a descriptive adjective or adverb. There would usually be an objection, a lecture from the judge for me not to stray from simple declarative answers, apparently modifier-free.

In his opening remarks Giffin made a veiled warning to the jury that underneath my attractive persona was something far less appealing.

The substance of my testimony did not differ from that of the first trial, but the staccato-like nature of Giffin's continuing objections left it somewhat truncated. I guess I had surprised them the first time around by being such a good *communicator*.

Halfway through my testimony as we approached my description of that fateful day of demotion, Judge Stevens changed his ruling and said he would allow part of Ridge Shannon's conversation. I was allowed to say I'd been told I was too old and too unattractive, but not that I wasn't deferential. Dennis objected, but to no avail. When I finally was asked, I simply said "too old, too unattractive, and something else I'm not allowed to mention at this time." It was hard not to be mildly petulant at moments like that.

When Giffin got to my former brief labor woes at KEYT, the judge acted surprised, as though he hadn't heard any of this before. He had clearly allowed Giffin to bring it in, without ruling on our earlier mention to have it excluded.

True, it referred to a different time period than the November 1980 slot to which we were being forced to limit *our* evidence.

Giffin's tone was intimidating as he asked whether the fuss at KEYT had meant that I had been desperate to get out of there and had in fact been looking for a job?

My reply was an unhesitating "no"; the fact was that several months after my reinstatement, the competing station which covered Santa Barbara had wanted to hire me as their anchor. I had refused that attractive bid because I much preferred KEYT.

As we defused the issue of my past history and moved to other witnesses, I noted Sarah's growth in her courtroom abilities. In Kansas City she had been somewhat reticent when examining witnesses. Now she was calmer and totally unintimidated by either Giffin or Judge Stevens. Sarah knew her law as she always had, but now there was a self-assurance that could easily be detected even in her body language. On occasion, Giffin or Mark Johnson lunged forward with an objection. Sarah stood her ground, gracious but strong. When the judge would disallow certain vital specific testimony that he had allowed in the first trial, Sarah spoke up firmly; she would continue on with only the slightest pause, respectful but very determined.

During Bob Hamilton's testimony, I noticed that he, too, was more confident in describing how Metromedia had promised in negotiations not to change my appearance. There is something about being made to tell the truth twice; in the second telling, one just becomes more resolute. In one of his answers, Bob was able to make the unassailable point that at the end of my brief tenure, the ratings had shown Metromedia reaching number one for the first time in three years. Metromedia had been trying desperately to keep that information away from the jury. Thanks to Bob, they had failed.

When Giffin brought up Bob's phrase, *cause célèbre*, and worded a question to suggest that I had plotted all the publicity, Bob shot back, "I never said that. Please don't try to trick me." That was precisely what Metromedia's lawyer, Giffin, had been attempting to do, and at that moment his strategy became obvious to everyone in the courtroom.

The transparency of the judge's attitude was often reflected in the conversations held out of range of the jury's hearing. He warned Dennis that when the time came for the testimony of the psychiatrist I had consulted, no testimony should be related to sex discrimination or what he termed "the abused female syndrome."

It was up to Scott Feldman to provide once again some key testimony. At this point in early 1984, Scott was still under contract to KMBC, yet he no longer worked there. Brenda Williams and Larry Moore co-anchored the news. Since Feldman was actively looking for work, it was in his interest to offer a subdued approach to testifying.

Scott was light-hearted as he told of his role in our first audition tape together:

> Q: In that interview, were you playing a senator or something like that?
> A. Yes, some kind of political type.
> THE COURT: Which Senator?
> A. Senator Feldman.

Moving on from there, Scott gave good, incisive answers that mirrored most of what I had alleged in my claims.

But when asked what Ridge had told him on the fateful day when he had summoned me to his office, Scott weasled. Dennis merely read the transcript of Scott's original depositional equivocations. His presence in itself wasn't electrifying, but it opened up a revealing line of inquiry.

When they got to the issue of Pam Whiting, the attitude of the judge was seen in open court in the following exchange.

> GIFFIN: Mr. Feldman, from your observation of Ms. Whiting, was it your feeling she could have used some help in the area of makeup and appearance?
> FELDMAN: Strictly my personal opinion?
> GIFFIN: What was that?
> FELDMAN: I thought she could have—I don't know how to put this.
> GIFFIN: Phrase it as delicately as you can.
> THE COURT: There is an immunity that applies to witnesses in court, Mr. Feldman.
> FELDMAN: I thought she needed a little help on makeup and clothing.

I could hardly contain my anger at Giffin's admonitions on delicacy. Had anyone, I wondered, ever told him that he needed help with his makeup? I felt like adding another bump to his nose, ever so delicately, of course.

Judge Stevens dismissed Scott with a cheery, "All right, Senator, I guess you are excused."

Reaching into our winter bag of tricks, we brought out a new witness to bolster the damages claim of our fraud charge. Psychiatrist William V. McKneeley was a professor at the University of Kansas Medical School. He had made a psychiatric examination of me and was prepared to testify that my experience had created a clear reactive depression, one that kept me away from many social contacts, with induced hair-loss, colitis, and neck pain.

Metromedia fought to keep Dr. McKneeley's testimony

out, preferring instead to present their own expert testimony from some doctor I had never even met. At least McKneeley was colorful, using such language as "scumbag" to describe how I'd felt after the demotion.

Then it was time for the return engagement of R. Kent Replogle. He had already checked into the Holiday Inn under an assumed name.

This time around, limitations that Judge Stevens had placed on our evidence and the diminution of the many facets of the original charges into just part of one charge kept Replogle off the hook. I noted that he still looked apish as he tried to pooh-pooh the importance of Nielsen ratings, which had started to rise even before the focus groups began.

The judge had taken the unusual step of conducting a Saturday session and when it was completed, we had a much-needed day of rest.

This trial was being represented by all the officialdom of the court as a full trying of my fraud case. It was nowhere near that. That Sunday at Mass, Dennis and I directed special thoughts on the ultimate questions of right and wrong. Let the jury see somehow that this was an exercise in judicial manipulation. It was made all the more maddening by our inability to present the comment that had launched the whole mess.

If they hadn't told me I didn't defer to men and was being removed because of it, I might not have proceeded with the litigation. Mass was calming with its evocation of larger themes and higher judgments.

On icy Monday morning, one of our regular jurors was unable to continue, because of his emphysema. One of the alternates stepped in to take his place.

Then Pam Whiting stepped up for her second round of testifying on my behalf. Outside, a freezing rain raged against the windowpanes of the courtroom, the drops punctuating the soft-spoken answers that Pam began to give to Sarah's questions. Once again, the judge's limitations on any evidence other than that directly relating to the period of time I had been hired kept another witness from giving crucial testimony.

Giffin worked up his best accusatory expression when he confronted Pam with a little fact the defense had discovered. Yes, said Pam, she had cared about appearance enough to have her teeth capped.

Pam finished her second mortification by saying she had resigned from Channel 9, her self-confidence shattered by Metromedia's fanatical emphasis on appearance.

From the reading of Sandy Woodward's earlier trial testimony, the Joplin jury learned that I had worked hard while co-anchoring at Channel 9. Sandy was quoted as having said: "I think she fit in well, liked working with us, very friendly, very kind, very generous with herself and her time and her willingness to be sensitive to the situation other people were n, in that news room when we were depressed."

Sandy also had told of her own feeling of being "pushed to the wall to get a news program on the air" when forced to put down work and try on clothes for the media consultants.

She vindicated my own perception that the standards for dress at Channel 9 eliminated any expression of personality or individuality outside of a narrow range. A polyester bowed blouse and puce blazer fit the bill perfectly.

I was beginning to feel a little better as some of our fraud evidence began to get in.

On the lunch breaks, the town of Joplin was jumping. All the downtown restaurants had stand-in-line business. This city of forty thousand people, situated at the crossroads of Oklahoma, Kansas and Arkansas, hadn't ever seen such an invasion of the media. Local merchants were delighted with land-office business. Under a crisp blue sky icicles hung from their awnings.

Even the telephone company had new customers. Since the federal building had no pay phones, reporters collectively had new lines installed in a special press area beneath the courtroom.

If some had thought that moving the trial to Joplin would curb media interest in the case, they were only partly correct. It was still a mob scene.

Every move we took was taped, photographed or noted. It amused me that when I applied for a short term library card and checked out two books, my choices became front page news in the local paper, *The Joplin Globe*. As it turned out, I had time to read Gore Vidal's *Duluth,* but I never even got to start Philip Roth's *The Anatomy Lesson.* Still, belonging to the Y and having a library card made me feel a little more at home in this very strange situation.

It was a media circus. What do you do when you have to wait too long for the unwinding of things in a courtroom? You start doing goofy stories. For example, everyone noticed that one of the reporters, Susan Wiese of WCTN in Minneapolis, could have won a Christine Craft lookalike contest. Of course, I thought she was very attractive. On the day when we both wore long-sleeved maroon silk blouses with black wool skirts, we drew many a double take as Susan took her place, sitting directly behind me in the cramped courtoom at one of those little student-type writing desks.

Radio deejays came up with a makeup concept: "You can wear the same makeup Christine was forced to wear. And if you buy during this special offer, we'll hire someone...to come to your house, slam you in a chair and force the stuff all over you!"

A few blocks down the street from the courthouse, enterprising people at the Sugar Creek Designs Inc. were busy printing t-shirts and caps to commemorate the event. I was given all the different slogans in every color and size. Because they were genuinely positive (albeit a little crude) I tried not to take offense. Actually they were pretty funny: "Every dog has her day," "I survived the Christine Craft trial," and "K-9 versus Channel 9."

After much Metromedia protest, Dr. Sal Arria, my chiropractor from Santa Barbara, was finally allowed to take the stand. As I listened to his testimony of his treatment of my neck woes, I wished he could give me a quick adjustment right there on the spot. Sitting through endless days of court procedure had left me inflexible at best.

Sal, who treated many of the world's Olympic track athletes, practiced in Santa Barbara, where many of them live. A fine and conservative healer, he could show you how to cure yourself and prevent injury.

I had gone to him for various problems for years and he had seen me when I first pulled back into Santa Barbara from Kansas City, a stressed-out wreck with nervous neck spasms that he had helped me to endure.

Metromedia's witness to counter Sal was a Kansas City neurologist I had never seen before. I guess they call that diagnosis from a distance. He claimed that my neck pains would have subsided if they had been caused by my demotion. Clearly he didn't know what he was talking about.

Readings from consultant Lynn Wilford's deposition reiterated an important point that hadn't emerged in the first trial. Before I had ever gone to Kansas City, Media Associates consultants thought I wouldn't succeed because my appearance wasn't conservative enough for the Midwest. They had communicated this belief to Metromedia, but not to me. All of this was ironic because Media Associates had provided the original tape of me as a good co-anchor prospect.

Even the judge remarked off the record that he hadn't remembered Lynn Wilford's testimony as being so damaging to Metromedia the first time around.

Dennis and Sarah fought tooth and nail in an attempt to be allowed to read critical designated portions from various depositions and trial testimony. Through it all, they remained constant in their uphill battle to present our case.

Thankfully, a point of diminishing returns is reached when one side (Metromedia) objects so overtly and so strenuously. After a time the jury began to wonder why the defense was constantly leaping to its feet. The jury began to have internal questions about what they were not allowed to hear. Or at least that was my impression. Even Judge Stevens noted as much at the bench: "This jury is going to go home mad."

By this time, finally realizing it was useless to be angry at the severe limitations being imposed on us, I let myself be amused by an exhibit that had not surfaced at the first trial. It was a sheath of notes made by Ridge Shannon in his original search for a female co-anchor.

With his years of journalistic experience to provide criteria for measuring candidates, Shannon had written about one woman: "classic star, honest, not a bad reporter, needs direction; in person, horsey, big, double-chins...she is ugly, but has it on camera."

On my first evaluation I'd been categorized on the basis of my "feathery hair, some sparkle, fair voice and interpretation, no real sparkle." Later on in the process I'd rated another notation, "super references, excellent features."

Another woman in her second evaluation was, "Mexican, no beauty, experienced, 32." Another was "a knockout, classy, some stumbling." His candid notations revealed more about the selection process than his claim that he had carefully ascertained, as a first priority, the candidate's reportorial and writing abilities.

To avoid the stumbling that had occurred in the first trial, Ridge, sitting at the defense table, had been privy to all the prior testimony. Now with his wife in the courtroom (once again her eyes raised heavenward), he played his part as the chief defense witness.

Giffin elaborated heavily on the theme of Shannon's background, asking his witness to give endless details of such accomplishments as his own invention of "exit polls" during a Youngstown, Ohio, mayoral race in the late fifties. Listening, I wondered why that achievement was something to be proud of. To this day, I'll never know what relevance it had to the time period during which I was hired, the time period to which the judge restricted our own evidence.

Once again, Ridge characterized himself as a "priest, problem-solver and father confessor." He swore he had warned me about consultants in our very first telephone conversation. He also swore again I had told him that in Santa Barbara sometimes I just slipped out of the surf and on to the news set without makeup.

Dennis let Ridge ramble on, Giffin leading all the way. I knew Dennis well enough to know his silence and lack of objection was not out of frustration, but rather calculated to give Ridge enough of the proverbial rope.

Soon to be hung by his own inconsistencies, Ridge cast a soulful look at his wife, who was by now deep in her traditional prayer-like trance mode. With fascination I watched Dennis reel in the rope. There were many discrepancies between the deposition, first and second trial testimonies. Dennis brought up one after another, hammering home the question, "Which answer is correct, Mr. Shannon?" Stammering and stumbling, Ridge could only attempt to justify the inconsistencies by giving answers in which he sought to incorporate all the different statements. According to Ridge Shannon, telling someone her jaw was too square or one eye the wrong size and that both had to be changed was not an attempt to make them over. The divergency of his answers emanated an aura of unreliability. Ridge was pathetic, a burr-headed chameleon in horned rims.

That night in candid conversation Dennis and Sarah revealed to me that their law firm had been reluctant to allow them to proceed in Joplin. Certain senior partners let it be known that Giffin, Stevens and Metromedia had us just where they wanted us. When they counseled that we just abandon all hope, that there was no way we could win, it was only through Dennis and Sarah's persistent reminders to their bosses that *they* had not heard the evidence, that we got the company's permission to continue. I realized I'd made it this far by the skin of my teeth.

The next day the defense droned through more medical

testimony from people who had never met me or treated me. Because they were members of the same Kansas City social club, one neurologist had been asked by one of Giffin's law partners to be a defense expert in the trial.

When the time came for the closing arguments, Giffin chose to sanctify Ridge Shannon, the quasi-priest news director. "This is indeed the trial of Ridge Shannon," Giffin intoned. "He is the one who stands accused of having lied to this plaintiff. It is his honesty, his integrity, his reputation which rests in your hands."

If there had been any misrepresentations, Giffin would argue, they were just "little lies."

But Dennis would have a chance to remind the jury what those "little lies" had been. He offered: "A great lawyer once said that the truth doesn't fly in the room like a winged bird; it has to be dragged in by its heels, kicking and screaming."

Getting Replogle and Shannon to admit inconsistencies in their prior testimonies had been grueling; still Dennis had succeeded.

His statement wasn't eloquent, but it sure worked: "They wanted a $100,000 house. They got what they believed was a $50,000 fixer-upper. But they didn't tell Ms. Craft they regarded her as a $50,000 fixer-upper."

I had never conceived of it that way. Dennis had presented a powerful analogy. My plaster may have been crumbling, but my spirit was intact.

After a mere three hours of deliberation, the jury returned and my spirits soared again. The jury found against Metromedia and assessed damages at $225,000. Giffin argued that any punitive damages were inappropriate because the case involved individuals, rather than the corporation, alleging, "It was just two people acting in Kansas City."

After another hour, the jury returned with an additional $100,000 in punitive damages. At that moment, one of the reporters gave me a Joplin High School neck pendant. Dennis, Sarah and I walked out into a light snowfall to meet the press.

In just five months, we had successfully tried and won two trials. Yet Judge Stevens and Metromedia had gotten what they wanted, too. By drastically limiting both our case and our evidence, they had seen a jury render us a lesser dollar award than in the first trial. For some reason, though, both Stevens and Giffin looked pale as the verdict was read. There were no gracious congratulations from Giffin this time around, just an icy stare and a statement to the media that "It was a shock to me, followed by a large sense of personal failure."

As the hordes of reporters began asking their questions, I noted several people in the crowd wearing the latest style of Joplin millinery. It was a cap that read, "Sic 'em, Christine."

To those folks, my comments were simple, "It's no fun being the world's ugliest anchorwoman, believe me. But I have, I hope, some sense of continuing integrity. The more they do this, the stronger I get, thank God!" Then I gave a thumbs-up sign to someone I recognized in the crowd. The click of a battery of shutters carried that image across newspaper front pages the next day. My eyes looked very tired.

Dennis and Sarah prepared to drive back to Kansas City, where they would be toasted and cheered by a large group from the law firm. We had, it turned out, surprised a lot of people.

I collected my stack of t-shirts and hopped into a rent-a-car to drive the one hundred miles back to Tulsa. There I caught a jet for L.A.

It was close to midnight when my dad picked me up. In the back seat Brinkley barked with excitement as he saw me. I reached to scratch his ears. "When this is all over, a rhinestone collar for you, baby!" I told him.

As we drove out of L.A. descending down the grade into Camarillo through orange groves closer and closer to Santa Barbara, my dad and I chuckled at the reports on CBS radio. "Is that a voice I know and love?" asked Dad. Sure enough, it was. But my soundbites were followed by the statement of a

Metromedia spokes*woman*. They would certainly consider an appeal. How much longer would this go on?

I had no answer for that, but I did know one thing. It had been an even greater victory in Joplin than in Kansas City. Rope us, tie us, kick us, we still win.

I found myself humming, "Oh, no. They can't take that away from me," as Brink and Dad and I drove past my favorite surf spot, Rincon, glimmering in the January moonlight, three foot glassy and mechanical, just begging to be ridden at the crack of dawn.

9.

THE JOPLIN VICTORY had one particularly pleasant aftereffect—it made me less hermetic, more self-confident, and less reluctant to engage in social intercourse. Right there when I needed him was my best friend, Paul Lindhard.

A sculptor whose art had entranced me for nearly twenty years, he also bore the dubious fortune of being the best-looking man in Santa Barbara. On matters ranging from art to politics to love, Paul always provided a visionary perspective. We had a special irreverent communion that never seemed to fade.

I could be completely loose with Paul. There was no dress code in the mind of our relationship. We helped each other out. I took special joy in writing proposals for his public sculpture commissions all over the country.

I had the love of the truest, sweetest friend, without being "in love" with anyone. Paul and I had always been very sensual with each other with episodic periods of sexual renewal, but neither one of us had made the mistake of being at all possessive. Paul was a vital, positive force in my life, and with luck he would remain so. Most nights, though, I was one of the seventy percent of Americans who admit letting their dogs be bedmates. Brinkley didn't mind at all. I wondered sometimes if I'd ever have the desire to be fully involved with someone again.

To help bypass the *angst* of that question, I acquired a second dog, Daley. Named after the famed Olympic decathlete, Daley Thompson, my new dog was a stunning puppy mixture of high-strung Rhodesian Ridgeback and black Great Dane. Unfortunately, even two and a half years after the fact, the mutt remarks were still stinging. Running down a fog-shrouded low tide beach with my own two muttskis loping in and out of the sea helped me keep my balance.

On the legal front, as with the first verdict, Metromedia was unwilling to accept the result of the second trial. They petitioned Stevens to order yet another trial, but he declined to do so, perhaps fearing the ridicule of his peers. They then filed an appeal with the Eighth Circuit Court. In order to stay in the game, we cross-appealed on all three issues, asking the higher court for reinstatement of our first fraud verdict, our first jury's sex discrimination verdict, and a retrial of the equal pay act claim which we had lost.

Three justices of the Eighth Circuit would consider arguments and briefs from both sides and then issue their verdicts at some indistinct time in the future. The only higher court in the land was the U.S. Supreme Court. It would be a year and a half after the Joplin victory before we learned what the Circuit Court would rule. I fervently hoped that the appellate ruling would not be only favorable, but that it would spell the end to what was rapidly becoming a melodrama. Being Joan of Arc was pretty tedious stuff.

I had learned that the name of the game was clearly "How much justice can you afford?" My lecturing allowed me to stay in the fray longer than most people could have. But what of the average American with a legitimate Title VII action? How could he or she possibly afford to stand up and challenge discrimination, especially when practiced by a powerful corporation? Existing laws were not sufficient to protect certain basic unalienable rights.

I was in that sort of mindset when coincidence and opportunity collided. Gary Hart's presidential campaign in Iowa asked me to participate in some forums with the Senator, as he stumped before the caucuses in that state. I was not being asked to endorse Gary Hart, but they did feel that the issues of my fight were germane to the Senator's point of view. One of the strong themes for those who listened to his "new ideas" campaign was the importance of equity of opportunity. He was waging a grass-roots strategy for votes in the first electoral test of the eight Democrats who sought the presidency.

Participating in the forum at Drake University were three other women: Minette Dodderer, an Iowa legislator who had introduced a comparable bill in her own state; Dottie Lynch, chief pollster for the Hart campaign; and a farm activist wife with plenty to say about how Administration policies affected farm women.

Like Hart, all of us agreed that one proper role of good government was to be active in promoting the reality, not just the rhetoric, of justice for all.

After spending time with Hart, I was convinced that he believed at the core of his political and personal philosophies in workplace equity and promotion on the basis of merit, not to be denied by sex or age or race. He had understood at once that the real issue of my case wasn't whether or not I was young or old, pretty or ugly. He knew that the issue of "deference to men" was a type of discrimination endemic to the American workplace. He felt it was a practice that should not be acceptable in our great country.

Though I generally considered myself a non-doctrinaire sort of Democrat on most things political, surely on the question of sex discrimination the Democratic party offered more interest in finding the solution. Ronald Reagan, on the other hand, offered a latter-day "Uncle Tom" as chairman of the Civil Rights Commission. The ultra-conservatives thought government should deregulate itself right out of the civil rights business. There were more important things to spend our money on. Pershing missile deployments and star wars research do not come cheap. Women would have to sacrifice claim to their full right in the name of the national interest. And while we were at it, the Reaganauts warned we had better not terminate unwanted pregnancies or we'd be dubbed murderesses.

Whew! Women had worked so hard to get the few rights we

had in controlling our bodies and our lives; why should we be willing to give up ground just to maintain a male hierarchy? Collectively we had to hold on with all our might.

Since I was no longer working as a reporter, I could exercise my first amendment right to free speech. As I became more politicized, I was finding a direction that offered public dialogue and hope. On the lecture tour, I did not omit political themes from my speeches. Further work with the Hart campaign led to my emceeing his big rally in Union Square in San Francisco. I did some speeches at the State Democratic Convention, and some speeches for an Assembly candidate in California's Eighth Assembly district where the incumbent was the notorious sexist, wine king Don Sebastiani. When the California legislature had voted to pay tribute to astronaut Sally Ride, Sebastiani had voted no, stating that "the only way women should go into space is with a one-way ticket."

Back in Santa Barbara, I could now be involved in the local issues I had reported on for so many years. For example, I was on the side of those who would see certain criteria met at the Diablo Canyon Nuclear Power Plant before they fired up the thing. It sits on top of an earthquake fault and was built in part by some two hundred workers under the influence of angel dust. The Nuclear Regulatory Commission had wavered on the decision to grant it a test license. Then there were oil companies with plans to build more platforms, processing plants, tanker terminals, and storage facilities up and down our coast and deep into our forests. My support went to a citizen's initiative which would have kept those facilities consolidated with minimum marine tankering. I walked precincts for our mayor, who wanted to serve on the Board of Supervisors, and did TV spots for a judicial candidate, who had championed the homeless. I was also keeping busy writing pieces for the *Santa Barbara News & Review*.

Invited to address a small college in Marshall, Missouri, I was asked by a member of the audience what I thought of President Reagan. "He's probably a really nice guy to go riding with up at the ranch," I answered. Then an eighty-six-year-old woman with blue hair stood up in the back of the auditorium and called out to me, "You'd mean you'd go horseback riding with that sexist son-of-a-bitch?" The audience exploded with laughter. Momentarily, at a loss for words, I finally answered her with, "Yes, but I'd have him ride side-saddle."

I had learned never to underestimate the depth and the breadth of feminist sensibility. It occurred in every locale I visited, with women of all ages, races and occupations. It was an earthy, internal understanding that fueled all of us to try and make things better. If each individual could in her own life create a non-sexist environment, evaluating individuals on their merits rather than on their gender, that way of life might become the larger reality.

I had been particularly struck by Metromedia's claim that it was primarily women viewers who had disliked my age and appearance. "Women of your own age group, Christine, your peers!" Ridge Shannon had "shared" that finding with me. The conclusion drawn from my own experience of grass-roots American feminism led me to focus on a change in consciousness for all those who came to hear my lectures: "If it is true that we women snipe and bitch and rip each other to shreds, then it is time for us to STOP IT immediately. It is no longer acceptable to be our own worst enemies. To be anything less than cohesive is just plain dumb."

When time for the Democratic Convention came in July 1984, I had landed a job anchoring Convention Television or CTV, the official video newsmagazine of the party. Our hour-long program would be shown twelve times through the day with a fresh new program each of five mornings. Receiving it would be a highly select, captive audience of top politicians, fellow journalists, and key opinion makers in my own field. Convention Television would be piped into 15,000 hotel rooms via closed circuit and would reach most of the delegates to the convention. I anchored a team with an impressive crop of reporters including Jody Powell, Barbara Matusow (author of *The Evening Stars*), Chuck Conconi (*Washington Post*), Jack Germond (*Baltimore Sun*). I worked with a terriffic crew from the Kamber Group, a political consulting firm from Washington that produced the program. It was exciting to work with the medium again, especially with such top-flight pros. The convention itself offered us so many stories, great speeches on the convention floor, great moments in history, great food, great parties. The peak moment for me came when I was quick-exiting a portable washroom. There, out of the men's facility, came my broadcast hero, Bill Moyers, and we ran right into each other. He had seen our program and had some encouraging words that I would not quickly forget.

The Mondale selection and the election with its predictable result came and went. When on earth would we know the Eighth Circuit Court rulings?

Different sources had described the court to me as all-male and politically diverse. One liberal, one moderate, and one conservative. Would this perhaps be the culmination of centrist opinion that I had first sought in coming to the Midwest?

AT THE FIRST of the year (January 1985) there had been an interesting development relating to the treatment of women on-air employees at Channel 9. Brenda Williams filed a sex and race discrimination complaint against Channel 9, against its current owners, the Hearst Corporation, and its former owners, Metromedia. She did not comment to the media about the case. She hired Dennis to represent her and the affair was quickly settled out of court for a reportedly healthy sum. Brenda also bargained to stay on the air as the KMBC co-anchor until another contract year had expired. A road had been paved, at least for Brenda Williams.

Metromedia offered to settle with me for $100,000, less than half of what our legal costs had been. I refused.

On the night of June 27th, I got a phone call that our

appellate decision would be handed down in the morning. Paul spent the night in anticipation of wonderful news.

At 7 A.M. Pacific Standard Time, the phone rang and Paul reached out to give my hand a squeeze. I picked the receiver up and heard Dennis's familiar voice and Sarah's too, though less clearly. They both asked if I could hear them. Then with the utmost clarity Dennis said, "Brace yourself! It's bad news, kid." His declaration was followed by a protracted moment of silence. Then both Sarah and Dennis asked in near unison, "Are you there?" They were perhaps worried that I'd keeled over. But I hadn't. The black-robed bastards had done it to me again. As Dennis put it next, "They took it all away, dear."

Once more, this time without feeling, I asked why? Citing various paragraphs of the opinion, Dennis explained that these three men didn't feel there was enough evidence for a "reasonable" jury to conclude there had been fraud. The jurors had been "unreasonable," in the judges' opinion.

I thought of the jurors in Kansas City and Joplin. They had not been frothing feminists or civil rights activists. These had been Midwestern, middle-class, grass roots people—foreman, schoolteacher, beautician. I reflected back on the tedious selection of twelve sequestered jurors in Joplin. If anything, those people had hardly been inclined to award a large sum of money to anyone. But both juries, after observing the demeanor of witnesses and the presentation of all the evidence, had awarded damages, both actual and punitive.

I remembered Judge Stevens's somber posturing as he told the juries after their verdicts, "Now you are through making decisions. And I thank you for your services in this case. It has been an unusual case and an unusually long case and I think it is a significant case. There is no other way, I don't think, short of military service in the United States, to serve your country any better or any more honorably than on juries in this Court." He didn't tell them that their hard work and their decisions might be deemed absolutely worthless.

The opinion of the three-man panel had been written by John R. Gibson, a friend of Judge Stevens, with offices in the same Kansas City building and, like Stevens, a new Reagan appointee.

With those facts in mind and considering the general anti-civil rights vigor of new court appointees, Gibson's opinion wasn't unexpected. But the shock this time came from the fact that the two judges who could have overridden Gibson did not. Judges Donald Lay and Theodore Macmillian had penned their names to the curious opinion as well. Supposedly reasonable men, what had prompted them to throw out the product of eighteen unanimous jurors as wasted and misdirected efforts? I wondered if they had even bothered to look at our appellate brief or at the record.

The Eighth Circuit opinion referred to its findings, "having considered the evidence in the light most favorable to Ms. Craft, that there was no sex discrimination...there was no fraud...there was no improper squelching of evidence on equal pay issues." In the light most favorable to me, there had been no case?

As Dennis told Joe Henderson of the *Kansas City Times*, "The law was applied by two unanimous juries who found sufficient evidence to award punitive as well as compensatory damages. These juries heard all the evidence and were not handicapped by the dry, lifeless record on appeal."

Stunned as I was by the fateful phone call, when the opinion itself arrived by express mail the next morning, I was positively apoplectic.

It read like the Metromedia brief. Its thirty-one pages bore only passing resemblance to my experience at Metromedia or to the case that had been established and decided before two different juries of my peers. Seized by genuine anger, I read testimony attributed to me that was not mine, but rather the defendant's. The justices Gibson, Lay, and Macmillian were not only taking everything away; they were doing so by putting words in my mouth. Dennis and I were determined to challenge this farcical opinion. He drafted a petition for rehearing by a full panel of the Eighth Circuit. It read in part, "The seventh amendment to the United States Constitution declares:

> In suits at common law, where the value in controversy shall exceed twenty dollars, the right of trial by jury shall be preserved, and no fact tried by a jury shall be otherwise reexamined in any court of the United States, than according to the rules of common law.

The three-man panel opinion handed down in this case simply is in fatal conflict with the Seventh Amendment. Three members of the Court have put their name to an opinion which violates all rules of appellate review enshrined in the decisions of this Court and the Supreme Court of the United States, by attempting to resift, reweigh, reexamine and redetermine factual issues on plaintiff's Missouri common law fraud claim, despite two lengthy trials in which eighteen jurors, fairly chosen from cross sections of the two Missouri communities of Kansas City and Joplin, already have personally heard, seen, examined, sifted, weighed and determined the factual issues as the Constitution directs they—and only they—must do. Judicial integrity and conscience compel reinstatement of Craft's jury verdict."

Dennis concluded: "Perhaps no one has stated the principle underlying jury verdict review more eloquently than Judge Arnold (also of the Eighth Circuit):

> Occasionally verdicts may be returned with which judges strongly disagree. This is a price, we think, worth paying for the jury system, which is embodied in our Bill of Rights and sanctified by centuries of history. When questions of fact are involved, common sense is usually more important than technical knowledge, and twelve heads are better than one.

"Or three. Rehearing or rehearing *en banc* is requested on all issues." The Eighth Circuit responded with a terse sentence: they wouldn't bother to rehear.

Of course, we could never know what had gone on behind those closed doors of higher jurisprudence.

Considering that only seven percent of the country's federal judges are women, was it possible that these men were merely speaking for the male power structure? Nowhere were many men about to let women claim workplace equity without one hell of a struggle.

Of course, we could only guess at the rationale for the opinion. Still, Dennis and I knew we had to try to exhaust all remaining legal recourse. I was not about to quit. Even though the United States Supreme Court only hears about four percent of the cases that come before it, we would ask them to hear ours. The Supreme Court is nothing less than the last voice of the people for justice.

In the meantime, having suffered the appellate loss, I thought that public opinion might be less favorable to me. To my amazement and delight, such was not the case. People who heretofore hadn't cared much about women's rights or TV news, nonetheless balked at double-jury verdicts being shuffled into insignificance.

People of diverse political backgrounds offered support, both emotional and financial. Through the National Organization of Women's Legal Defense and Education Fund, the Women's Institute for Freedom of the Press, and through journalism instructor Bob Picard at Louisiana State University in Baton Rouge, tax-deductible avenues were provided for their generosity.

There was a need. The first trial had cost $23,000 in out-of-pocket expenses, which I had met. The second trial had racked up another $26,244.11, which I still owed. The appellate and Supreme Court pleadings would only tack on more obligations.

Looking to the future, Kathy Bonk, creator of the Women's Media Project, established a Women's Media Fund in Washington. The idea was that women winning sex discrimination media cases would put some of their settlements back into the fund to establish a revolving financial source for the next group of women needing early help. In that spirit, I spoke at fundraisers in New York and Washington along with a terrific speaker and inspiring congresswoman, Pat Schroeder of Colorado.

There were some other cases in process. Cecily Coleman, for one, claimed she wanted to go to trial against ABC with a compelling sex harassment case. Cecily alleged that she'd been manhandled by one of the corporate executives. She had been a junior exec herself, in charge of the ABC News/Harvard Voter Project. She claimed that when she went to network personnel asking for protection from the harassment, they told her not to worry, they'd take care of it, and then they fired her.

Elyssa Dorfman, a sales executive at CBS radio in Philadelphia, also claimed her network would not protect her from the sexually abusive language and actions of a salesman.

Gloria Gibson, Metromedia's ex-anchor of Washington D.C. station WTTG, had just gotten permission to file her federal sex and race discrimination claims against Metromedia.

There was a maternity-based demotion case already filed by an anchorwoman in Topeka.

Then there was a young woman from Duluth, Minnesota, who had been ordered to do weathercasts with two microphones. Each was placed prominently on each breast, just above the respective nipples. Apparently too young, too pretty, and too deferential, she has nonetheless finally balked and filed sophisticated federal harassment and discrimination charges.

Whatever the merits of these particular cases, a message had been sent to the broadcast industry, which they would ignore at their peril.

As Los Angeles star KABC anchorwoman Christine Lund put it, "A bell once rung, cannot be unrung."

I took heart from what a number of journalists had to say. My all-time favorite anchorman, John Chancellor, gave a great speech at a national convention of the Radio, Television News Directors Association (RTNDA). He told them something they certainly did not want to hear. As he travelled across America, he found the proliferation of warm, cuddly "communicators" at most of the nation's TV stations a little disconcerting. They were, he said, "all so young, so agreeable, their style of reporting so *bloodless!*"

I was bemused that at that very same Las Vegas convention, panel discussions were held on "The Craft Decision." Members of the RTNDA didn't think of asking me to give my side of the story. I would have gladly. You had to understand that these were people infinitely more interested in management than in journalism. Listening to tapes of their panel discussion, I never heard a single news director speak up for addressing the root problems of sexism or ageism. All they seemed to care about was how to word their discrimination without getting sued, and how to avoid "bad apples" like Christine Craft.

Cecily Coleman settled her case with ABC on the first day of trial for what AP reported was a cool half million. The newspaper reported that Elyssa Dorfman was half as successful at CBS. Both defendants were furious that the settlement amounts had been leaked to the media. I wondered, though, if all the settlements would make a difference, if the real patterns and practices of discrimination would simply remain unadjudicated and hidden by semi-secretive financial agreements.

The major part of the support that really bolstered me up and kept me going did not come from organized groups at all. It came from individual men and women. Substance was still more important than style to many people, and they cared enough to say so. They told me not to quit, not just in this litigation, but in general. And they offered me examples of why it was important to see things through to their legitimate conclusions.

A city councilwoman from Fresno, California, remembered

her own term as a weekend anchor in that city. Out-of-town consultants told her station management that she was "too serious" and should spend her time tending to her "disheveled hair and dangly earrings."

Karen Humphrey's letter had one passage which really struck home:

"I still feel pain from that parting, even though I wouldn't return to TV for all the tea in China. But most of my pain now is not for myself. It's for you. . . and for all the serious, caring, talented women journalists whose futures in TV news are limited by 'consultants' and the managements who live by them. It's for the poor little misled actress types who are thrust into anchor positions because they supposedly have 'charisma,' but who never become professionals and may never have any real personal identity. It's for the current women anchors whose overscale salaries are less than those of the men who sit beside them because station managment finally found a way to pay discriminatory salaries in spite of union wage scales, and federal law. It's for the kids who want to go into TV news that think it's somehow more noble than the other branches of entertainment. And most of all, it's for a medium which has so much promise and which could live up to its potential for making Americans the best informed people on earth, except that it has sold out to the consultants and marketing experts and salespeople."

One former Santa Barbara viewer offered another more lighthearted perspective: "Unfortunately there are some odds we can never overcome—like our inability to grow a beard to hide a receeding chin (or a square jaw) or a mustache to camouflage a short upper lip, etc. If you've ever seen Kris Kristofferson or Tom Selleck without their facial hirsute adornment, you know what I mean. Keep your powder dry and your anima intact!"

Another viewer, Jon R. Rutherford of Kansas City, was delightfully blunt: "When I first saw you in your co-anchor position on Channel 9, I didn't care for your delivery; but as the days went on I came to understand that what disturbed me was that, unlike many reporters, you were using your intelligence. That has kind of a shock value on TV! I became a kind of fan, then an enraged fan when you were terminated. Hardly a day has passed since then that I haven't thought about what I considered the very raw deal you got.

"To hear that two juries agreed with me was sweet music to my ears. It was almost enough to make one feel there was some justice in the land."

Jessie Delahanty wrote from West Haven: "All the women out here are in your corner. Only last week I mentioned to my husband that men newscasters were of many age groups including fat, bald, woven hair, hair pieces, nervous twitches, gray, pockmarked, etc. Yet they go on, gaining prestige along the way."

Women's routes to prestige were different. Venerable CBS News had named as its most prominent female anchor, Phyllis George, a beautiful sweet gal who, to her credit, never claimed to have been a reporter. Executives at CBS wanted her "star" quality because she had been a successful Miss America and hostess on "NFL Today."

Over at ABC News, the most visible woman news anchor, Kathleen Sullivan, had limited reporting credentials and described herself *(TV Guide)* as a "good communicator, who just loves world affairs." Her rapid rise in TV journalism was credited by insiders to ABC News president Roone Arledge's appreciation for the nuances of "sweater girls."

I kept hoping to see her do a tough interview or a field piece on a complex subject, something to warrant the loftiness of her anchordom, but I was to watch and wait in vain. Meanwhile the genuinely competent female correspondents at ABC were not getting the same recognition for their achievements as their male counterparts. Surely Anne Garrels, who spoke Russian and did the best reporting of any American network correspondent in Moscow, deserved a position of journalistic authority. Her field pieces from Central America were the clearest and the gutsiest of anyone's. She would not be rewarded with anchor ascendancy. I guess she was far too qualified. Variations on the same theme applied to Carole Simpson, Rita Flynn, Sheila Kast, and many others.

Perhaps it was just symptomatic of the times. That year there had been a sociologically telling Miss America contest, held unsuccessfully to erase all memory of Vanessa Williams, who was discovered to have posed for sexually explicit photos in *Penthouse*.

Both Miss Utah, the next year's winner, and Miss Ohio, the first runner-up, who was discovered to have on her record a shoplifting charge, had television ambitions. Posed in her bathing suit, thighs pressed together so as to create the appropriate allure, Miss Utah responded to the question of what she wanted to be when she grew up: "Oh...an anchor-woman, or perhaps a White House co-res-pon-dent."

Look, out Sam Donaldson, Bill Plante, and Andrea Mitchell, here she comes...Miss America.

Then Miss Utah, the eventual winner, was asked the same question. She too wanted to be an "anchorperson." Miss Utah, advertised as an intact Mormon, leveled with the American public, telling them she didn't support the equal rights amendment because she was "a woman."

Spike heels clicking and buttocks in gear, they both walked off the pageant stage heading directly for America's newsrooms.

More letters revealed that what had happened to me was far from unusual. From Iowa, another female anchor wrote she had discovered that her co-anchor was making 45% more than she. "To date, that has never been rectified. I could file a complaint with the Iowa Civil Rights Commission. But instead, I have chosen to get completely out of the business because of the trends I see in broadcast journalism... appearance over intellect."

I had a number of letters from people in broadcasting who had actually filed EEOC charges only to settle out of court, usually because they were too poor to proceed. All of those people were left with a hope that someday someone would stick it out.

Another woman anchor wrote to thank me for "taking this first momentous step that will encourage all women to fight back when they are degraded and humiliated in this cold and cosmetic business."

I found that I served as a good example even to women I did not agree with on a number of other issues. For example, this letter came from Arizona: "I am not a champion of the 'right to choose' movement as it has been applied to homosexual rights or abortion. The trail you blazed is what equal rights for women is really about. Issues like yours will gain the support of the millions of women ERA has lost through their insistence on embracing secondary and unpopular dogmas better decided by court decisions. Nice gain!"

On the flip-side of all the positive input, I was literally floored by a quote which seemed to doom me to an eternal blacklist. It appeared ironically enough in an issue of *Ms.* magazine. In a cover edition devoted to the progress of women in TV news, mention was made of the Craft case. Discussing how to deal with the pervasive breed of sex discrimination and sexual harassment that still permeate the broadcast workplace, Nina Totenberg, a radio correspondent for National Public Radio, advised, "You can either take it like we all do, or sue like Christine Craft and never have a career."

I phoned Ms. Totenberg, determined she should understand that I had *resigned* from my Santa Barbara job. She spoke of her support for my stand, but added that she had talked with her friends who were women executives at the networks. They had seen my work during the er to ask her friends to please refrain from putting me on any blacklists, until I asked to be there.

The whole incident was reminiscent of Metromedia's pointed comments to me that it was the women viewers in Kansas City who didn't want to give me a chance.

Maybe there was the resentment factor operative in all this. I had dared to say "hold it" to sexist practices to which most proed to hold every position of real power in the network superstructures.

Jane Pauley, the "Today Show" anchor, put it extremely well to the *New York Post*: "Christine Craft has made television executives publicly accountable for private attitudes that should have been retired ten years ago."

Out into the limelight came the statistics from the Women's Media Project. During a month's viewing, of 576 stories filed by network correspondents, 517 were done by men, 59 by women.

Among the three networks, there was a seven point difference in the percentage of women reporting stories.

CBS Evening News	14.7%
ABC World News Tonight	8.4%
NBC Nightly News	7.9%

Overall, only 10.2 percent of news stories were filed by women, an increase of merely three-tenths of 1 percent since the U.S. Commission on Civil Rights reported similar findings in 1974-75 data.

Analyzing the status of women and minorities on television, it was easy to deduce that both were best described as "Window Dressing On the Set" (U.S. Commission on Civil Rights, 1977).

Of anchorpeople over forty in this country, 97 percent are male, the remaining three percent are fortyish women who don't look their age.

The doyenne of television newswomen, Marlene Sanders of CBS News, encouraged other women to strive for equitable treatment. But she acknowledged she did not think "women are going to be allowed to get fat and jowly and bald. People say to me, 'Gee, you're still here.' Well, I don't look my age (52)."

When I found the data just too depressing, I grabbed for my last resort mood-elevator. It was a Hallmark card, sent by a Kansas City supporter, with a big bunny dancing on the front and the music of "Zip-e-dee-do-dah" playing when you opened it up to read "Hang in there!"

On the legal front Dennis had good news. Thirteen Yale law students were doing a study for us and for the NAACP on appellate review. Just how common was the practice of throwing out jury verdicts on fact issues? And wasn't that practice in direct conflict with the Seventh Amendment which guarantees the right to jury trial?

What our Yale students found in their survey of appellate reversal was a shocking trend that affects all individual citizens. The erosion of a jury's constitutional position as fact finder was certainly not isolated to a mere handful of cases. The law students found that in the last year the Federal courts of appeals had considered 233 cases in which a party challenged the correctness of a jury's verdict; the appellate courts reversed the challenged verdict, in whole or part, in 105 cases. Thus 45.1 percent of the time the appellate courts conducted their own unconstitutional reexamination of the evidence, disagreed with the verdict of the jury below, and substituted their view of the facts for that of the jury.

In almost all the 105 reversals the district judge who presided at trial had sustained the very verdict with which the appellate court has disagreed. In our case the situation was even more magnified. During the course of *two* trials the same district judge had ruled the evidence of fraud sufficient for the jury no less than six emphatic times. This was the same judge whose sex discrimination findings were found to be impervious to attack by his friend writing opinions for the Eighth Circuit.

In the Yale study, the appellate reversal rate did not include cases in which a jury verdict was overturned because of purely legal issues, such as the correctness of jury instructions or the admissibility of evidence.

Even more alarming was the discovery that the appellate courts had not reviewed, with an equal degree of overzealousness, verdicts favoring *all parties*. The current pattern of appellate fact-finding would represent an intolerable disregard for the commands of the Seventh Amendment regardless of whether the burden of that constitutional infraction fell equally on plaintiffs and defendants alike. But it did not. On the contrary, the courts of appeals had been far more likely to overturn a verdict if the jury found facts favorable to the plaintiff.

The students charted:

REVERSAL RATE BY PARTY: ALL CASES

JURY VERDICT IN FAVOR OF	REVERSAL RATE
Plaintiff	51.0%
Defendent	20.0%

Other numbers pointed to another inescapable fact. If you were a single plaintiff who had won a jury verdict on a constitutional issue, you stood a less than 30 percent chance of having that verdict upheld. If the litigation had to do with discrimination, the higher courts would uphold jury results only 44 percent of the time.

Some of the other data showed that if we had been in the Ninth Circuit Appellate Court (California, Washington, et al.) we would only have had a 9 percent risk of having our verdicts overturned. However, the Eighth Circuit took the liberty of reversing juries 57 percent of the time. At the very least, appellate justice was not meted out equally across the land.

The U.S. Supreme Court was supposed to be the ultimate determiner of constitutional guarantees. Dennis's Supreme Court brief summed up our position at this last stand in the battle. As earlier in both trials and in every written statement, his plea captured our gut feeling.

> This case represents the highwater mark of a tide of appellate overreaching that has, in many circuits, largely usurped the historic and sacred fact finding authority conferred solely on civil juries by the Seventh Amend-

ment. Thus, this court should grant the writ to restate the established line of demarcation between judge and jury's function—which will enhance efficiency in the administration of justice and restore public faith in the certainty of every person's constitutional right to civil jury trial.

This court's history as vigilant guardian of the constitutional right of all litigants to have a jury determination of factual issues is rich indeed. As this case starkly exposes, however, and as the following review of recent appellate decisions strongly suggests, unbeknownst to the citizenry and to this Court, the constitutional right to a jury decision of fact issues in civil cases is being eroded, and the established history and binding precedent of this court is being brazenly ignored to the point of obliteration, or relegation to a mere footnote in the history of constitutional jurisprudence.

The NOW Legal Defense Fund gave us the $5,000 that it cost just to have the Supreme Court brief printed in a special typeface. They paid for our hotel rooms in Washington, D.C., and flew us in so that we could at least climb the steps of that marvelous building with all our documents at the ready for the clerk's certification, and with our heads carried high. No one would ever say we were quitters.

The night before, I told Dennis that even if the weather was a howling blizzard, we had to deliver our petition right to the Supreme Court's door. He heartily agreed, and the next day, in the still chill of 10 degrees, we approached the marble columns and the entranceway, step by step. Their elegant whiteness was etched against the bluest, coldest sky. We felt about as pure as you can get.

I had to fly home that night, for the next day I would begin packing all my possessions. I was moving out of Santa Barbara, leaving my beautiful home behind.

I had taken a television anchor job at probably one of the smallest TV stations in the country, independent KRBK in Sacramento, the California capital. The station's newsroom was a trailer. I knew that there would be few problems with prima donnas in a trailer. There's just not enough room for grand exits and entrances.

    I was beyond flat-broke and needed to get to work. Besides, I missed the pace of a newsroom. Since the station was just creating a newscast and since it had limited technical and human resources, the anchors would be editing, writing, reporting, as well as reading from a teleprompter. At the very least, I'd be busy doing things other than thinking and talking about myself when the Supreme Court's decision finally came down.

10.

I HAD DONE A whole hell of a lot more in ten years in television news than just be a litigant. And so, when I set about investigating the possibility of returning to TV, there were a few hopeful signs.

My notoriety had at least gotten me in the door at KNBC in Los Angeles, KPIX in San Francisco, and KOVR in Sacramento. In the Bay area as a speaker for a state district attorney's convention in Santa Cruz, I dropped in at my old station, KPIX. The current news director, Bruno Cohen, told me that I looked good on tape but that his consultants had determined that the longest on-camera women's hair permissible was chin-length. Mine was actually skimming my shoulders. He already had two very successful anchorwomen, both with hair just touching the chin. He didn't mention what hair length was demanded for female reporters in the field—the position that interested me.

In Sacramento, where I was giving a speech to an affiirmative action group, I had been asked to appear on a public-affairs program at KOVR, the ABC affiliate. While at the studio, I asked if the news director would see me about job possibilities in the state capital. California has arguably the most volatile and interesting legislature in the country for a reporter to cover. I certainly qualified as a political junkie.

News director Al Jaffe sat in his see-through enclosed office, peering out at the newsroom through dark glasses. He didn't say much, just a mumble here and there, enough to make me sure he was only numb, not dead.

I realized that probably no news director in his right mind would tell me if there was a blacklist. I sensed I had struck fear in almost all their hearts just by having challenged certain things at one particular station. I suspected they were also curious to see me, this woman who had dared to fight the system. But they overlooked the fact that because I had been willing to risk the unspeakable—never being on the air again—I had won a definite freedom from certain of their ilk. I would not bow and scrape to get a job, and I wouldn't defer to bogus superiority. I knew that genuinely competent news directors were a scarce and dying breed.

It was a decidedly upbeat moment when the news director of Sacramento's tiniest television station called me, unsolicited, asked if I would be interested in applying for the anchor job on a brand new newscast. UHF Channel 31 had tried to do news a year earlier with a skeleton staff and had failed to draw a self-supporting audience share. It was abruptly taken off the air, but now the station planned to cut its losses and regroup.

The owners, Koplar Communications, brought in a risk-taking new general manager, New Yorker Ed Karlik. They re-assigned the anchor-reporter of their St. Louis station, John Schutte, to be the news director. He would have to put together all the elements for a local news broadcast that would, hopefully, be a success. The company decided to invest six figures, and make a more concerted commitment to local news and serving the community.

I'm sure they felt that my national name recognition might draw new viewers to a station that was watched less frequently than any other in town. They also were scared to death that I might be a litigous type who would sue anything that moved at the slightest provocation. They just didn't know me. Like most people, they had formed their impressions from the half-truths that had so often characterized the coverage of my lawsuit.

I agreed to meet them in Sacramento to see what they had to offer. In my quieter moments I began to reflect on the emotional challenge it would be to subject myself once again to the nightly scrutiny endured by all anchors. I had been a good soldier in fighting for my rights, but would I be strong enough if someone else called me a mutt, again? Was I a fool for even considering going back? I had my own breed of reluctance that conflicted with the attraction of returning to the invigorating atmosphere of a newsroom. I just didn't want to set myself up for more wounds to the psyche. One rape of the spirit had been enough.

It was in that cautionary spirit that I went on a two-day whirlwind tour of major cities in New York state. I had been asked to speak on the anniversary of women's suffrage about current civil rights restoration bills pending in Congress and about the administration's plan to dump affirmative action guidelines. The tour was sponsored by the New York State NOW and included a rousing rally at Manhattan city hall. Bella Abzug, Carole Bellamy who was running against Ed Koch for mayor, and former national NOW president, Judy Goldsmith, all gave moving speeches as to why we must all remain alert to attacks on workplace equity. I gave my personal account of the deficiencies in existing law to a cheering crowd. In all my lectures in halls big and small, nothing had been more exciting than this big apple audience. They were well-informed, political, passionate, and there was nary a heckler in the crowd.

Fresh from that rhetorical triumph, we squeezed into a NOW member's car and drove to the Nassau county courthouse for another in our series of rallies. After I spoke, I went into the building to get some water, followed by an intrepid AP reporter. After some perfunctory inquiries about the limbo-like state of my case, she asked if I thought I had been blackballed in TV news. I told her that I had just begun to look for a job and didn't really have enough data yet to come to that conclusion I told her I had been approached by one California station about a possible anchor position; so I thought blackballing might be too harsh a term. She became insistent, wanting to know which station, where, how much they were offering to pay me and whether I had accepted the offer. I told her that it had merely been an inquiry, that I hadn't even been interviewed, and that I didn't want to jinx the opportunity by being too specific.

By the time I got off the train in Poughkeepsie three hours later, a swarm of local reporters showed me the AP story that had gone out over the national wire. "Christine Craft says she may have an anchor job at a big California station" read the first line. I had to spend the next two days explaining things to reporters who covered us in each of the remaining cities I visited. When I got home to Santa Barbara, my home town paper featured my picture and the overblown news item. I couldn't imagine why anyone would care whether I had signed on to another news job; all the commotion over the rumor that I had been approached was unbelievable. By the time I flew to Sacramento a few days later, the interest hadn't waned. As I stepped out of the commuter hopper from Santa Barbara, there on the front page of the *Sacramento Bee* was another picture (at least four years old) with the bold print question, "Will Christine Craft join KRBK?"

As I shook hands with the news director and general manager, I imagined they were cringing inside. Although they professed to understand the publicity barrage that accompanied my case, I knew they were feeling more unsure of what they might be getting into.

But they weren't the only ones who were wary. The station was quite small, located next to a Ramada Inn, with an aging trailer for a newsroom. With plans for an absolutely bare bones staff and with cameras, decks and tripods literally on their last legs, I knew it would take a super effort just to get a newscast on the air, much less draw a sizeable audience reaction without at least a year of solid work and building of the reportorial and technical staffs. It would be a whale of a job, or as *Entertainment Tonight's* Jeanne Wolfe would later put it to me: "Do you have some sort of penchant for lost causes?"

But, by God, I liked the new director and general manager.

We went to a Sacramento restaurant and, over fresh fish and fine California wine, we all put our respective cards on the table. They were looking at several candidates and were inclined to take a risk and offer me the job. But their corporate bosses didn't want any bad apples in the bottom line bin. Who knew what Christine Craft might do if miffed over some slight perceived as sexist? It might be a living hell to have an enraged feminist as the main spokesman for your station, one you feared to remove from your airwaves because she might sue the hell out of you.

Their positon was totally logical. For my part, I needed to be convinced of their commitment to news. How can you cover the legislature as well as the multitude of news events in the nation's twentieth largest city without enough troops and tools? They conceded that it would be a minimalist effort, at least at first. They had hired a bright, rapid-fire sportscaster from Illinois named Rich Gould and were already out doing stories to put in the can for the upcoming new newscast. An avant-garde weatherman with blond good looks and a penchant for the bizarre had been hired out of the Louisiana market. Pat Flanigan used his brains and his comic tendencies to construct videos, not news clips. His use of the medium would be entirely different from the rest of the newscast, and, as such, provide an entertaining note.

They were looking at several male anchor candidates, including a handsome young man who had been a magazine co-host for a nationally syndicated program, doing segments out of Des Moines, Iowa. Tim Klein had served four years at WHO-TV, the station whose radio affiliate had once employed Ronald Reagan. He had an endearing manner and a quality of genuineness that came right through the lens.

They apparently had auditioned several women anchor candidates and had even looked at a tape of Brenda Williams. But they had been most taken by a young beauty from Fresno with a great wardrobe and by me.

My resistance to taking the job centered on a real question

of whether or not I could deal again with the pore-by-pore nightly scrutiny and whether I could do a respectable job with limited gear in the field. I wasn't sure how to answer the eventual offer. I talked to my best news director ever, Carol Breashears, in Los Angeles, who put it to me straight, "If you don't take this job, you are a fool. You have to get back in the business and show everybody that you can still do it, regardless of the station, or the size of the station. You will do the best with what there is, and you will know it and others will know it. You are a journalist and you are meant to be a working on-air journalist."

If I still felt a soupcon of hesitation in making the decision, Brinkley and Daley pushed me over the edge. The crumbled remains of an empty forty-pound bag of dog food stood near their feed bowls. When you gotta take care of the kids, you've gotta work. I was soon on my way to Sacramento to scout out a new nest and meet my co-anchor human and the rest of the "31 News Tonight" team.

The station scheduled a press conference where we were all introduced. We had met each other just a few minutes before. It seemed too good to be true, but we all got along incredibly well right from the start. I was the oldest member of the team by a good seven or eight years. There was only one other woman in our newsroom, Jami Harrison, a red-headed senior reporter who covered everything and anything. Winner of California running marathons, Jami is diligent, responsible, reliable, and extremely nice.

Rounding out our staff is Rory O'Farrell who does ski reports, great outdoors pieces, and producing, editing and switching. He is the one person retained out of the original newsroom. Bill Bailey, an older man, does one weekly feature called "Good News," pieces about unusual people like a young woman massage therapist who gives comfort to dying AIDS patients. Our resident Mensch is Derek Bang, a gangly, well-informed and well-spoken movie critic. Our head cameraman, Gary Greenich, a crazy cowboy who always shoots straight, provides a beautiful smile and an easy laugh along with his quality work. It is an unusual group, a sort of renegade team made stronger by the presence of three good interns who contribute just for the experience of working in a newsroom. Some of them undoubtedly will go on to good careers in television. Finishing off the whole package is a fantastic, brand-new set that was built specially for the new newscast. It is pricey, functional, and as good or better looking than anything else in town. Despite my initial reservations, I soon saw that working at KRBK was going to be as much fun as it was challenging.

My surfer/reporter pal, Patti Pannicia, accompanied me on the tedious house-finding trek along the coast from Santa Barbara and then inland to Sacramento, fondly referred to by locals as Sack of Tomatoes, California. It was in the middle of the coldest cold snap in local memory, daytime temperatures topping out at thirty-eight degrees.

Somewhat depressed at the rotten weather and what I'd seen so far of the local topography (dense tule fog), I began the search for a neat place for me and my dogs to live. Scanning the classifieds, I zeroed in on one ad that read, "Absolute Privacy, secluded, fenced half-acre, close-in yet rural, has own corral." An hour later, I was meeting my new landlord and surveying my new little house, calm oasis surrounded by acreage, horses, ponies, fruit trees, and a creek down the slope from the back yard. Brinkley and Daley would survive and so would I.

Actually all the major life changes were the best thing that could have happened to me while I waited to hear whether or not the Supreme Court would hear our Seventh Amendment claim. I was so busy with the logistics of moving, and getting used to an exciting new job, and keeping my dogs from digging out from under the chain link fence, that I didn't have time to dwell on IT anymore. The less self-absorbed I could manage to be, the better.

There was always the reminder that the Supreme Court

was too busy to hear more than four to six percent of the cases that came before it. Dennis and I knew that though we had exposed a gaping flaw in the system, simply because the work load of the Supreme Court is so great, it is a battle against staggering odds just to capture the highest Court's attention. Abusing the Seventh Amendment has become common practice for most federal appeals courts throughout the land. A sense of misguided justice is inflicted with impunity. We could only hope that the Supreme Court would be moved by the troubling implication that appellate court judges who have never seen or heard one word of the trial under review are engaging in wholesale reevaluation of the subtle credibility and other factual determinations that can only be made by the jury after full and complete personal observation of all the evidence.

I still had hope when I read our brief and its mention of Justice Rehnquist's past eloquent tributes to the right to jury trials in civil cases.

> ...from the dissent in *Parkland Hosiery Co., Inc.* v *Shore* 439 U.S. 322, 337-356 (1979): "...maintenance of the jury as a fact-finding body is of such importance and occupies so firm a place in our history and jurisprudence...any seeming curtailment of the right to a jury trial should be scrutinized with utmost care.

If Justice Rehnquist followed his own lead and looked at my case with "utmost care," he would have to vote to rehear it. It was such a glaring example of denial of the right to be judged by one's peers.

There was a huge press assault on me once again as we debuted our newscast. CBS Morning News, ABC, and *Entertainment Tonight* all did interviews and stories. ABC News sent correspondent Ken Kashiwahara who remarked as he left for his next assignment that the piece would probably air the following night, "barring some national tragedy."

The next morning the shuttle Challenger exploded.

Our second newscast was that evening. Indeed, the whole

first month we were on the air was a time of extraordinary news. The worst flooding in California recorded history shut Sacramento off from the rest of the state, as levees on two major rivers crumbled and cofferdams were swept away. Thousands were evacuated, many lost everything. We knew that in times of natural disaster, viewers turn to the network affiliates for their news, to the stations with the helicopters and the state-of-the-art live gear. We knew we didn't have the tenure in the market to expect people to watch us to find out whether their house would soon be swept away.

But we did a credible job at the ten o'clock newscasts through three weeks of critical storms and unimaginable flooding. Dressed in serious rain gear and hip waders, sloshing through flood zones with a cameraman recording the devastation, 31 News Tonight was on the scene, even renting helicopters when needed. The anchors did not hesitate to go out in the field. We were sort of the Avis rent-a-car of TV news. We tried harder. And all of us were proud of the results. We had shown that we could do a competent job covering a major story with wide local impact night after night, even though we'd just gone on the air and had some gigantic technical problems at first.

I was being kept so busy, I didn't even get hung up on what I looked like on camera. I was caught up in the excitement of events and the full-time job of recording them. Sacramentans were incredibly supportive and warm, sending me flowers, cookies, cards, letters, good wishes, telling me always that I looked wonderful, inviting me to meet them, to speak at their civic groups.

The world heated up even more as the Philippine drama unfolded. I stood in the newsroom reading AP copy, as the stories broke from Manila where Corazon Aquino and the Philippine people sent Marcos flying into exile. It felt great to be plugged in once again to the heartbeat of the global media. You could never get the whole story, but you could get some of it, sometimes fairly truthfully. I found that I read the wires more critically than I ever had before my own legal battles, having seen so personally the ongoing tension between illusion and reality, and the control of the weak by the powerful.

My adventure had given me new political awareness and a desire to report the news meticulously. I knew too well what it was like to be misquoted. Journalism is one of those professions where the more you do it, the better you are. You start to learn what and who really makes things tick. You can't get there without time in the trenches. Through a somewhat unique route, at forty-one I felt I had finally arrived.

Sacramento houses the capital of the state. Dashing under its dome, tripod and tapes in hand, I raced to cover the governor's State-of-the-State message. KRBK, being a local station, had been given a fine press area, almost as good as the L.A. stations. It was thrilling to see the full assembly of legislators and then to pull several of them out of the crowd after the speech for our cameras. Speaker Willie Brown, minority leader Jim Neilson, School Superintendent Bill Honig, all these powerful state leaders were available for comment, accessible for the asking. I realized my Sacramento experience would leave me knowing a great deal more about California legislative politics, a subject in which I had a burgeoning interest.

My days were packed full in this treasure trove of a news town, where you can find a lobbyist or a representative of every movement or corporation or ideology for any story you want to do, with people not at a loss for words.

As much as I miss the beauties of Santa Barbara, the mountains and the sea are close by here. Lake Tahoe and San Francisco are both in our backyards. My neighbors are a Palomino and a quarterhorse, Fancy and Coco. There are ponies, too, and I go through lots of carrots staying a good neighbor. I am meeting some incredible people, like California Supreme Court Chief Justice Rose Elizabeth Bird. The station encouraged me to do a series of reports on her difficult reconfirmation bid. I started reading her actual opinions in the law library and found huge disparities between what her opponents say she says and what she really says. It is a complex topic, dealing in part with the heavily emotional issues of the death penalty and women on the bench. My brain is busy and my faculties are fully challenged by this investigative work. I love this job and I don't regret the time out necessary for me to fight unfair practices in the media. I still get hundreds of letters from women all over the country telling me I've won already, for all of us.

I've always thought, win or lose at the U.S. Supreme Court, this case would be at the very least, a snapshot of a moment in history. It catches the image of an American woman refusing the straightjacket that sexist TV industry would force upon her, and it symbolizes the actions and aspirations of an entire era.

EPILOGUE

ON MARCH 3, 1986, the U.S. Supreme Court declined to grant cert in the case of *Craft* v *Metromedia*. Justice Sandra Day O'Connor, only female on the Bench, was the only member of the Court to decide in favor of hearing the case. On that same day, Christine Craft was honored with a resolution by the California State Senate praising her for "outstanding achievement in journalism and perseverance and courage in her convictions."